A recipe not shared will soon be forgotten.
When it is shared with others,
it will be enjoyed by generations to come.

We wish to extend our sincerest Thanks
to all our friends and family members
who have encouraged and supported
us throughout the creation of this book.

With love,
Kelsey & Sara

Table of Contents

MAD AT MARTHA

The Story of a Cookbook

by Marny Lifshen

Not all authors have glamorous and extraordinary stories behind the creation of their cookbooks. Take, for example, Kelsey and Sara, two thirty-something friends in Austin, Texas, who fancy themselves good cooks and charming hostesses. Kelsey, a consummate entrepreneur, is the founder and CEO of two companies with many business and community responsibilities and little free time. Sara spent ten years in the hotel industry and is now a stay-at-home wife and mother of two little girls, juggling a crazy schedule while managing the household budget. Both love to cook and often entertain friends, family and business colleagues in their homes, regularly hosting everything from small luncheons to lavish dinner parties.

So what inspired these busy ladies to write a cookbook? It's simple, really. A healthy combination of admiration, frustration and good humor.

Their story begins, innocently enough, in a local grocery store on a Saturday afternoon. Kelsey is having a few friends over for dinner that night, including Sara and her husband Thom. Kelsey decides to make a beautiful dessert, a frozen raspberry bombe, from a recent issue of Martha's magazine. The photo is impressive and the cool, light dessert looks perfect for a sultry summer evening. Kelsey, an experienced cook who is not easily intimidated, begins to gather the ingredients.

As she wanders down the aisles, she reads with surprise that the recipe calls for NINE pints of raspberries, at a cost of about $4.00 per pint. Kelsey, in a state of sticker shock, suppresses her irritation and reviews her options. She notices that blackberries are on sale for $2.00 per pint, and decides to improvise. She moves to the frozen food aisle in search of the raspberry sorbet, still trying diligently to follow the recipe. Ever tried to find raspberry sorbet at your neighborhood grocery store? Closest she can get is strawberry ice cream, so again, she improvises.

At home, Kelsey reviews the rest of Martha's 500-word recipe and finds, to her dismay, that the last paragraph directs her to chill the dessert overnight. Her guests are due to arrive in four hours and probably won't stick around until morning for dessert. Sara calls just as Kelsey is visualizing various ways to shred the recipe, and immediately detects the frustration in her voice. "What's going on?" she asks. "Oh, I'm just mad at Martha," Kelsey replies with a slightly hysterical laugh. Thus, the title of this cookbook was born.

Like most people who cook, decorate, garden or entertain, Kelsey and Sara respect and admire Martha and all she represents. But, they are also often intimidated by the sometimes (okay, often) unrealistic level of perfection she has come to personify. They have tried many fantastic recipes from her books and magazines, and share the feeling that you have to be an expert chef to follow the directions. They are normal people, perhaps like you, trying to reach the impossibly high standard set by their role model. Unless you grow and gather your own vegetables; bake everything from scratch; decorate with flowers cut fresh from your garden in a glass vase you've hand-blown; build, sand and stain your own dining room table; and use name cards with scented calligraphy and silk ribbon borders – you just don't measure up!

So, the question we ask ourselves is this: "Can you be a successful cook and even host parties WITHOUT an herb garden, an executive-appointed kitchen, a staff of professional chefs, a food stylist and a greenhouse full of Japanese eggplant and organic baby carrots? How about on a tight budget and on an even tighter schedule?"

Kelsey and Sara firmly believe the answer is YES! As a result of passionate conversations spawned by the "raspberry bomb incident," as it's now called, they felt compelled to compile a cookbook with simple, clear, user-friendly recipes that everyday people can use everyday. They have organized this cookbook to be truly easy, by using a font size that you can actually see and vocabulary you can actually understand, and including up-front tips and important facts like preparation time, serving size and recipe variations. They have also provided many choices and options in the recipes, everything from fresh versus dried herbs to alternative baking pans.

Kelsey and Sara have chosen 150 common but delicious recipes that they have collected, enjoyed and served for years. They are affordable, flexible and family-friendly recipes that are simple to prepare but will still impress your guests. And, as a little bonus, they have included wine recommendations with certain recipes.

You may be wondering if Kelsey and Sara are truly "Mad at Martha," but the answer is no. They are just among countless people in the endless pursuit of emulating Martha while still living in the real world.

About the Authors

Sara Singer

Of all the rooms in my home, the kitchen is my favorite. To me, food equals love; love for my family and friends (for whom I often cook) and love of creating something that looks, smells and, of course, tastes great. From casual picnics to beautiful holiday meals, I like to cook them all. Even though I now feel very comfortable in trying new dishes, it wasn't always so. My confidence and success have come from plenty of trial and error. I have learned many lessons along the way and expect to learn many more, but the important thing is that I always enjoy the experiences.

I was born in San Jose, California and moved to Austin, Texas in 1991 with my husband Thom. Although I worked as a catering manager for a large hotel, my personal culinary skills were limited. As young newlyweds, Thom and I couldn't afford to eat out very often, so we had friends and family to our home for meals frequently. In the beginning, I could barely coordinate baked chicken, white rice and steamed vegetables to all be ready at the same time, so for help I subscribed to a few cooking magazines and read dozens of cookbooks. After experimenting on Thom and a few of our more understanding friends, my skills and comfort zone grew, and I discovered that I really enjoyed cooking and entertaining. In fact, I now look forward to trying new recipes for my family, and to throwing parties, small or large. After ten years in the hotel business, I decided to stay home with my daughters, Jackie and Kate. If you think that leaving a full-time job gives me lots more time to cook and throw parties, think again! I still go to Martha's books and magazine regularly for inspiration and new ideas, but I don't hold myself to her somewhat impossible standards. After all, you don't see Martha mincing seven different kinds of fresh herbs with a five-year old who wants to play Chutes & Ladders and a six-month old who needs a diaper change!

I believe that anyone can be a successful cook and host – trust me, I'm not an expert, so if I can do it, anyone can! My advice is to just start simple and keep practicing with new recipes whenever you have a chance. Try to keep in mind that the meal should be about spending time enjoying the company of your family or guests, not fretting over a menu. Here's a tip: if you're slaving madly at the cutting board while your friends are sampling wine and sharing stories, something is wrong! Things may not always go as planned, as I've found on more than one occasion, but keeping a positive attitude helps. When minor tragedies do occur, there's not a lot you can do except laugh and learn from it.

Kelsey and I have compiled some of our favorite recipes which we have been enjoying and serving for years, and believe that anyone can successfully make. With this book, we hope you will be inspired to get into the kitchen and have fun creating something new for your next get-together. We have emphasized affordability, simplicity, flexibility, and of course, delicious taste in selecting these recipes. While I always try to use fresh ingredients, because I believe it really does make a difference, I'm certainly not opposed to short-cuts. In fact, I often buy mixed lettuce in a bag for my salads (since it's already torn into bite size pieces), baby-cut carrots (since they don't need to be peeled), and pre-made pie crusts, to cut down on the prep-time of some of my favorite recipes. Something tells me Martha would never admit to that . . .

Sara

Kelsey August

Okay, so the truth is more than one person has called me a "Martha Freak." I love to cook and entertain in my home. Sometimes it's a big group of friends to watch a football game, sometimes a romantic dinner for two, sometimes Sunday brunch for the family. As long as I get to try new recipes! The challenge has been trying to balance my busy professional life with my love for cooking for friends at my home.

I grew up in Ohio, and graduated from Ohio University in 1991 with a BA in Marketing. Ready for a change, I relocated to Austin, Texas and landed my first real job. But, the entrepreneurial gene runs strong in my family, and I soon left to start my own direct marketing and fulfillment firm, Lone Star Direct. I have grown my company over the past nine years into a multi-million dollar firm, and have assumed leadership roles with several community and professional organizations in Austin. In 2001, I took my passion for creating, developing and implementing positive company cultures and started my second company, WorkplaceToolbox. I've been lucky enough to make many friends through my businesses, and I enjoy having them to my home.

Good food has always been a part of my life; my mother was a gourmet cook and my grandmother was a master of everyday cooking. I've been preparing (and improving!) my family recipes for years. Cooking is a great release for me – a way to unwind from the stresses of running two businesses, and a way to let my creativity flow.

I've never been one to shy away from challenges, so I have tried many recipes and ideas from Martha's books and magazine. I have often found, however, that I have to spend a small fortune on the ingredients; practically be an expert chef to follow the directions; and spend a lot of time to complete even one recipe. I knew there was a way to host successful dinner parties on a budget and under a time crunch – because I've done it! So it was with excitement that I set about writing a cookbook with Sara. This project has enabled me to demonstrate how I have combined two of the things I love - cooking and business. Basically, I approach cooking the way I do business –

what is the most efficient, most affordable way to get me the best results? The way we organized our cookbook and the kind of recipes we included will certainly show my practical, business-like side. I believe that anyone with interest and patience can become a great cook who knows how to throw a terrific dinner party. Don't be intimidated by unusual recipes, or be afraid to try something new – you may find that you love the flavor of an ingredient you've never had before. Feel free to modify recipes, either for flavor or for health reasons – add grilled shrimp to a Caesar salad, for example, or replace cream cheese with light cream cheese. But don't eliminate all the fat, or you WILL eliminate the flavor! Finally, if you remember only one thing, remember this: Keep it simple! You don't have to use three separate bowls to combine ingredients if they'll all end up in the mixer together anyway, right? Not only will keeping it simple save you prep time, it'll save you clean up time! Something tells me Martha doesn't have to do her own dishes . . .

Kelsey

MAD AT MARTHA

Simpler Methods for Success in the Kitchen

Basic Pantry List

Aluminum Foil
Baking Powder
Baking Soda
Black Olives
Bread Crumbs - plain and
  seasoned
Canned Goods - broth (beef,
  chicken, and vegetable),
  diced tomatoes, refried
  beans, stewed tomatoes,
  tomato paste, tomato sauce,
  tuna
Chocolate Chips
Cocoa Powder
Cooking Spray
Corn Starch
Crackers
Flour - all purpose
Garlic (whole cloves)
Honey
Maple Syrup
Oatmeal
Oil - olive oil (extra virgin and
  light), vegetable
Parchment Paper
Pasta (dried) - any variety

Peanut Butter
Pepper (black)
Plastic Wrap
Plastic Zipper Bags
Red Wine - Cabernet
  Sauvignon and Merlot
Rice - white
Salt (iodized)
Soup - cream of chicken,
  cream of mushroom
Soy Sauce
Spices (dried) - basil, bay
  leaves, cayenne, chili
  powder, chives, cinnamon,
  cloves, curry powder, cumin,
  dill, ground ginger, mustard,
  nutmeg, oregano, paprika,
  parsley, rosemary, sage
Sugar - brown, granulated,
  powdered
Tea - any variety
Tortilla Chips
Vanilla Extract
Vinegar - balsamic, cider, red
  wine
Worcestershire Sauce

Basic Refrigerator List

Butter
Cheese (Cheddar, Gruyere,
    Mozzarella, Parmesan and
    Ricotta)
Eggs
Garlic (chopped)
Half and Half
Jelly
Ketchup
Lemon Juice
Margarine
Mayonnaise
Milk
Mustard
Produce - lemon, lettuce,
    mushrooms, onion, potatoes,
    tomatoes
Sour Cream
White Wine - Chardonnay and
    Sauvignon Blanc
Plain Yogurt

Basic Freezer List

Bacon
Ground Beef
Boneless Chicken Breasts
Coffee
Variety of Nuts - almonds,
    pecans, walnuts
Vegetables - corn, broccoli,
    spinach etc.

Equivalents

For liquid and dry measurements, use standard measuring cups and spoons. All measurements are level.

Volume

3 teaspoons	=	1 Tablespoon
1/8 cup	=	1 fluid ounce
1/4 cup	=	2 fluid ounces
1/2 cup	=	4 fluid ounces
3/4 cup	=	6 fluid ounces
1 cup	=	8 fluid ounces, 1/2 pint
2 cups	=	16 fluid ounces, 1 pint
4 cups	=	32 fluid ounces, 2 pints, 1 quart

Weight

1/4 pound	=	4 ounces
1/2 pound	=	8 ounces
1 pound	=	16 ounces

Miscellaneous

1 large egg	=	1/4 cup
7 - 9 egg whites	=	1 cup
12 -14 yolks	=	1 cup
1 lb. butter/shortening	=	2 cups
1 lb. granulated sugar	=	2 cups
1 lb. brown sugar	=	2-1/2 cups
1 lb. powdered sugar	=	3-1/2 cups
1 lb. all-purpose flour	=	4 cups
1 medium lemon	=	1/8 cup juice
1 medium lemon	=	1 Tablespoon zest
1 medium orange	=	1/4 cup juice
1 medium orange	=	2 Tablespoons zest

Interchanging Pan Sizes

Recommended Pan Size	Approx. Volume	Possible Substitutions
8 x 1-1/2 inch round baking pan	1-1/2 quarts	9 inch pie plate
		12 standard cupcake cups
		10 x 6 x 2 inch baking dish
8 x 8 x 2 inch baking pan	2 quarts	8 x 4 x 3 inch loaf pan
		11 x 7 x 1-1/2 inch baking pan
		12 x 7-1/2 x 2 inch baking pan
13 x 9 x 2 inch baking pan	3 quarts	two 8 x 1-1/2 inch round baking pans

When you substitute a different pan than the one recommended, it may be necessary to adjust the cooking time by adding or subtracting 5 to 10 minutes. Also, when substituting glass or ceramic for metal pans, reduce the oven temperature by 25° F.

Notes

Breakfast and Breads

Crustless Asparagus Quiche

A fabulous dish for a brunch!

1 lb. bunch (approx.) fresh asparagus
4 eggs
1/2 cup milk
12 slices cooked bacon, crumbed
1-1/2 cups Gruyere cheese, shredded
1/2 teaspoon salt

Preheat oven to 375° F. Cut asparagus into 1/2 inch pieces. Discard bottom 3 inches of stalk. Place asparagus in a steamer of boiling water. Cook, covered, for 5 minutes or until tender. Drain and cool. In a medium bowl, beat eggs. Add milk, crumbed bacon, cheese, salt, and asparagus. Pour mixture into a 9" pie plate sprayed with cooking spray. Bake, uncovered, for 30 minutes. Let cool before serving.

Serves: 6 - 8

Prep time: 30 minutes
Cook time: 35 minutes

ASPARAGUS : Stalks should be tender and firm and the tips should be close and compact. Stalks with very little white are the most tender. Asparagus toughens rapidly, so use as fresh as possible. White asparagus, while a novelty, is considerably more expensive than the green.

Banana Fritters

A great 2 inch treat for the kids. Or, arrange on a platter and serve them as an appetizer for a Brunch!

2 ripe bananas
2 Tablespoons water
2 eggs
1 Tablespoon margarine
1 cup all purpose flour
2 Tablespoons granulated sugar
1 teaspoon baking powder
1/2 teaspoon salt
1/4 teaspoon ground cinnamon
1/4 cup vegetable oil
3 Tablespoons powdered sugar

In large bowl, mash bananas. Mix in water, eggs, and margarine until smooth. In separate bowl, combine flour, sugar, baking powder, salt, and cinnamon. Stir dry ingredients into banana mixture. Heat oil in a skillet over medium heat. Drop batter by spoonful into hot oil. Turn once until browned, approximately 1-2 minutes each side. Drain on paper towel. Dust with powdered sugar.

Serves: 6 - 8

Prep time: 10 minutes
Cook time: 10 minutes

Blackberry, Peach & Oatmeal Crisp

This is wonderful "as is" for breakfast,
or served with vanilla ice cream for dessert.

1 package (10 oz.) frozen sliced peaches
1 package (10 oz.) frozen blackberries
1/2 cup granulated sugar
1-1/2 cups quick oats
1/2 cup firmly packed brown sugar
1/3 cup all purpose flour
1/8 teaspoon salt
1/4 cup (1/2 stick) unsalted butter, melted

Preheat oven to 350° F. Arrange the peach slices evenly in the bottom of a deep baking dish, then top them with the blackberries. Sprinkle the sugar evenly over the fruit. In a small bowl, mix the oats, brown sugar, flour, and salt together. Spread the mixture evenly over the fruit. Drizzle the melted butter on top. Bake, uncovered, for 35-40 minutes. Topping should be slightly brown.

Serves: 6

 You can also bake this in 6 individual ramekins, just divide everything evenly.

 Prep time: 15 minutes
Cook time: 35 - 40 minutes

24

Breakfast Casserole

This is great topped with fresh salsa.

1 lb. tube breakfast sausage
2 Tablespoons all purpose flour
1-1/2 cups whole milk (cold)
1 lb. frozen shredded hash brown potatoes
1-1/2 cups sharp Cheddar cheese, grated
3 green onions, finely chopped (white & pale green
    parts only)

Preheat oven to 350° F and spray a 9" x13" pan with cooking spray. In a large skillet over medium-high heat, cook sausage until just brown, breaking into small pieces, 5 to 7 minutes. In a small bowl, whisk together the flour and milk until smooth. Add this to the sausage, plus salt and pepper to taste, and bring to a boil. Reduce heat and simmer for 5 minutes to thicken sauce. Meanwhile, spread potatoes in the bottom of the pan. Top potatoes with 1 cup of cheese, then 2 of the chopped green onion. Spoon the sausage mixture atop this and finish with the remaining 1/2 cup cheese and last chopped green onion. *(This recipe can be done several hours or up to 1 day ahead to this point.)* Bake, covered, for 30 minutes, then uncovered for 15 minutes more.

Serves: 4 - 6

Prep time: 20 minutes
Cook time: 45 minutes

25

Overnight French Toast

As the name implies, this dish is perfect if you prepare it the night before you plan to serve it.

5 Tablespoons unsalted butter
2/3 cup firmly packed brown sugar
1/4 cup maple syrup
1/8 teaspoon ground cinnamon
1 loaf of fresh bread, such as challah or brioche
5 large eggs
1-1/2 cups half and half
1-1/2 teaspoons vanilla extract
1/4 teaspoon salt

Combine the butter, sugar, and syrup in a small saucepan. Stir over medium heat until the sugar has dissolved and the butter has melted. When smooth, remove from heat and stir in the cinnamon. Pour the mixture into a 9" x 13" pan. Cut the end off the bread loaf, then cut six slices, each 1 inch thick. Arrange bread slices in one layer in the pan over the syrup mixture. In a large bowl, whisk together the remaining ingredients and pour evenly over the slices of bread. Cover and chill for at least 8 hours, or overnight. In the morning, preheat oven to 350° F and bring the soaked bread to room temperature. Bake, uncovered, in the middle of the oven for 35 to 40 minutes, or until it is puffed and the edges are slightly golden. Serve immediately.

Serves: 6

 CHILL overnight or at least 8 hours

 Prep time: 15 minutes
Cook time: 35 - 40 minutes

Fancy Hash Browns

Martha would freak out. I make these hash browns with bacon on weekend mornings. I use the reserved bacon grease for frying. You can substitute regular cooking oil if you like.

1/4 cup oil or bacon grease
2 cups sweet potatoes, peeled and diced
2 cups russet potatoes, peeled and diced
1/4 cup yellow onion, diced

Heat oil or bacon grease in a large skillet over medium high heat. (You can use the same skillet from cooking the bacon.) Spread the sweet potatoes evenly in the skillet. Cook for 2 minutes, turning over often. Add the russet potatoes and cook 7 minutes, turning over often. Add onion and mix well. Toss for another 3 minutes cooking until golden. Season to taste with salt and pepper.

Serves: 4

If you cut off the root of the onion last, you will shed less tears.

Prep time: 10 minutes
Cook time: 12 minutes

Crustless Mushroom and Spinach Quiche

Made with Gruyere cheese, which is truly the best cheese for any quiche. I encourage you to try it. I know you will enjoy the flavor.

2 Tablespoons olive oil light
1/2 cup yellow onion, chopped
1 cup fresh mushrooms, sliced
1 cup fresh spinach leaves
6 eggs
3/4 cup Gruyere cheese, shredded
1/4 cup Cheddar cheese, shredded
1/4 teaspoon salt

Preheat oven to 350° F. Lightly spray a 9" pie plate with cooking spray. Heat oil in a large skillet over medium high heat. Add onions and cook for 1 minute. Stir in mushrooms and spinach. Cook for 3 minutes or until spinach is tender. In large bowl, mix eggs, Gruyere cheese, Cheddar cheese, and salt. Add spinach mixture and stir thoroughly. Pour into pie plate and bake for 25 minutes. Let cool 10 minutes prior to serving.

Serves: 6

 To cut down on cholesterol, substitute two egg whites stiffly beaten for each egg called for.

 Prep time: 20 minutes
Cook time: 25 minutes

 GRUYERE CHEESE (Switzerland): Light yellow body, tan crust. Mild, sweetish nut-like flavor, similar to Swiss cheese. Firm to hard texture, life span is 2 years. Used with fresh fruit, fondues, and fine cooking.

Pancakes

Martha would be proud – no box mix! All homemade, baby.

1 cup all purpose flour
2 teaspoons granulated sugar
1 cup milk
2 eggs
2 teaspoons baking powder

Here is an alternative technique for mixing: Sift flour into a medium bowl and stir in sugar. Make a well in the center. Add 1/2 cup of milk and eggs. Stir with a whisk adding baking powder and remainder of the milk. Let mixture stand for 10 minutes. Using a pancake maker or griddle (400 degrees), pour appropriate amount of batter and cook. The first side is done when small holes appear on the surface and the edges are lightly brown. Flip and cook second side briefly. Serve with butter, syrup, or honey.

Yields: 8, 5-inch pancakes

 Serve time: 30 minutes

Waffles

Top with fresh strawberries and whip cream. Or add pecans to the batter to give them a nutty flavor.

1-1/2 cups milk
2 eggs
3 Tablespoons oil
2 cups all purpose flour
4 teaspoons baking powder
1/4 teaspoon salt
1 Tablespoon granulated sugar

In a large bowl, combine milk, eggs, and oil. Mix well. Add flour, baking powder, salt, and sugar. Blend together. Coat waffle iron with cooking spray. Pour batter into waffle iron and cook 4 to 5 minutes.

Yields: 4 waffles

 Serve time: 30 minutes

Banana Bread

If you like bananas, I encourage you to add another one to this recipe. You'll love this bread!

1/2 cup margarine
1 cup granulated sugar
2 eggs
1-1/2 cups bananas, ripe mashed (3 large bananas)
2 cups all purpose flour
1/2 teaspoon baking soda
1/2 Tablespoon baking powder
1/2 teaspoon salt

Preheat oven to 350° F. In a large bowl, cream margarine and sugar together. Add eggs and mix well. Add bananas, flour, baking soda, baking powder, and salt. Mix thoroughly. Spray a 9" loaf pan with cooking spray. Pour mixture into pan and bake for 1 hour.

Serves: 12

You can always substitute pan size if desired. One 9" x 5" x 3" loaf pan equals one 9" x 9" x 2" square pan. If you use the square pan, you can rename this Banana Bread Squares. However, watch your cook time!

Prep time: 20 minutes
Cook time: 1 hour

Blueberry Muffins

A very berry delicious recipe! Great for anytime of the day.

1/3 cup butter
3/4 cup + 1 Tablespoon granulated sugar
1 egg
1/4 cup milk
1-1/3 cups all purpose flour
1 Tablespoon baking powder
1/2 teaspoon salt
2 cups blueberries

Preheat oven to 375° F. Spray muffin pan with cooking spray. In a large bowl, cream butter, 3/4 cup sugar, and egg together. Add milk, flour, baking powder, and salt. Mix thoroughly. Fold in blueberries. Pour batter into muffin pan, filling each cup 2/3 full. Sprinkle a Tablespoon of sugar on top of batter. Bake 30 minutes. After baking, cool for 20 minutes before removing from pan.

Yields: 12

 Prep time: 10 minutes
Cook time: 30 minutes

 CREAM: To soften a solid, especially butter, by beating it at room temperature. Butter and sugar are often creamed together until smooth and softened.

Catherine's Irish Soda Bread

This sweet bread is great for breakfast or as an afternoon snack with tea.

4 cups all purpose flour
1 cup granulated sugar
2 teaspoons baking powder
1-1/2 teaspoons salt
1 teaspoon baking soda
1/2 teaspoon cream of tartar
1/2 cup vegetable shortening (such as Crisco®)
1-1/2 cups raisins
2 cups buttermilk
2 large eggs

Preheat oven to 375° F and butter or spray two loaf pans. In a large bowl, whisk together the first 6 dry ingredients. Add the shortening, which will make lumps, then stir in the raisins. In a separate bowl, beat the eggs and buttermilk together. Add wet ingredients to the dry and stir with a large spoon or knead by hand (dough will be very sticky). Divide dough between the loaf pans and bake for 45 to 50 minutes. Let bread cool in the pans for 20 minutes before removing and slicing.

Yields: 2 loaves

Prep time: 10 - 15 minutes
Cook time: 45 - 50 minutes

Popovers

Even Martha would be proud of these popovers!

2 large eggs
1 cup milk
1/2 teaspoon salt
1 cup all purpose flour, sifted
1 Tablespoon unsalted butter, melted

In a large bowl, whisk the eggs and milk together. Add the salt and finally the flour, whisking until smooth. Brush popover cups (or regular muffin cups) with melted butter and fill halfway with batter. Place popover pans in the middle of a cold oven and turn it on to 425° F and bake for 20 minutes. Reduce heat to 375° F and bake for 5 more minutes. Quickly pierce the top of each popover with a knife or skewer and bake for 5 more minutes. Serve immediately or keep warm in the oven (turned off) for up to 5 minutes.

Yields: 6 from a popover pan, or 12 from a regular muffin pan.

 These are great for breakfast, served with soft butter and jam, or serve them as dinner rolls. This recipe refers to "popover pans" which have much deeper and larger cups than regular muffin pans, which is why they yield half as many.

 Prep time: 5 minutes
Cook time: 15 minutes

Margaret's Pumpkin Muffins

Kids love these year 'round.

1 can (15 oz.) pumpkin
1-1/4 cups (2-1/2 sticks)unsalted butter, melted
3/4 cup vegetable or canola oil
1/2 cup + 2 Tablespoons milk
2 large eggs, beaten
2-1/2 cups all purpose flour
2-1/2 cups granulated sugar
2 teaspoons baking soda
1-1/4 teaspoons salt
3/4 teaspoon (level) ground cinnamon
3/4 teaspoon (level) ground ginger
3/4 teaspoon (level) ground nutmeg

Preheat the oven to 350° F and line standard size muffin cups with papers. In a large bowl, combine the pumpkin, butter, oil, milk, and eggs. Beat well. In a separate bowl, stir together all the remaining ingredients. Mix the dry ingredients into the wet in batches until all is incorporated. Fill the muffin cups 3/4 full and bake for 20-25 minutes. For mini muffins, bake for 12 minutes. Muffins should be just lightly brown. Remove from pan and serve warm or cool on wire racks before icing.

Yields: 26 standard size, or approximately 6 dozen mini muffins

 Optional toppings: Once muffins have cooled completely, dust with powdered sugar or frost with our Cream Cheese Frosting recipe.

 Prep time: 15 minutes
Cook time: 30 minutes

Zucchini Bread

Yummy. Did I just use the word Yummy?

1 egg
1 cup granulated sugar
1/2 teaspoon vanilla extract
1/2 cup olive oil light
1-1/2 cups zucchini, grated
1-1/2 cups all purpose flour
1/4 teaspoon salt
1/2 teaspoon baking soda
1/2 teaspoon cinnamon
1/2 teaspoon baking powder
1/2 cup walnuts, chopped
1/2 cup raisins (optional)

Preheat oven to 325° F and spray a 9" loaf pan with cooking spray. In large bowl, beat egg and add sugar, vanilla, and oil. Add zucchini and mix well. Sift in flour, salt, baking soda, cinnamon, and baking powder into egg mixture. Add walnuts and optional raisins, and mix them in. Pour into loaf pan and bake for 1 hour. Cool for 10 minutes and remove from pan. Cool on wire rack.

Yields: 1 loaf

Prep time: 30 minutes
Cook time: 1 hour

Appetizers

Hot Artichoke and Spinach Dip

Serve with crackers or sliced baguettes.

1 cup Parmesan cheese, grated
1/2 cup sour cream
1/2 cup mayonnaise
8 oz. cream cheese, softened
2 garlic cloves (roasted if time permits)
1 pkg. (10 oz.) frozen chopped spinach,
   thawed & squeezed dry
1 can (14 oz.) quartered artichoke hearts,
   drained & finely chopped

Preheat the oven to 325° F and spray the bottom of a shallow baking dish with cooking spray. Combine all ingredients except the artichokes in a food processor and blend until smooth. Mix in artichokes and scoop mixture into the baking dish.
Bake, uncovered, for 30-45 minutes or until somewhat golden.

Yields: Dip for 8 - 10

Prep time: 10 minutes
Cook time: 30 - 45 minutes

PARMESAN CHEESE (Italy): This is a light yellow, hard and brittle cheese with a sharp, piquant flavor and aroma. Used mostly grated or shredded for seasoning soups, salads, casseroles, meats, pasta dishes, vegetables, etc. This cheese should be stored in a cool dry place and has a life span of 3 years or more.

Betty's Stuffed Cheese Puffs

Although this recipe calls for olives, these are also great stuffed with pecans, almonds, dates, or nothing at all.

1 lb. block sharp Cheddar cheese, grated
(don't use pre-grated, as it is too dry)
1 cup (2 sticks) unsalted butter, softened
1/2 teaspoon cayenne pepper
2-1/4 cups all purpose flour, sifted
1 jar (7 oz. net dry wt.) pimiento-stuffed small green
olives, drained

Preheat oven to 350° F. In a large bowl, knead all ingredients, except the olives, together until a firm, orange dough is formed, about 5 to 7 minutes. Take approximately 1 heaping teaspoon of dough and roll it into a ball in your palm. Press an indentation in the ball with your thumb and insert the olive. Cover the olive with the dough, reforming into a ball and place on an ungreased cookie sheet.
Note: If the ball is too big, the center won't cook all the way through, so keep them small.
Repeat until all the dough and olives are used. Bake for 12 minutes and serve warm.
Caution: Olives may be hot!
These can be prepared ahead of time, even frozen, and baked just before serving. If frozen, thaw before baking.

Yields: 6 dozen

Prep time: 30 minutes
Cook time: 12 minutes

CHEDDAR CHEESE (USA and England): Comes in white, yellow, or orange and flavors range from mild to sharp. Widely used in cooking, typically grated or melted. This firm cheese has a life span of 2 to 12 months.

Pecan Cheese Spread

Serve this spread with your favorite crackers.

1 cup sharp Cheddar cheese, grated
8 oz. cream cheese, garden vegetable flavored
8 oz. cream cheese, roasted garlic flavored
3 green onions, finely chopped
1 cup pecan halves

Allow the cream cheese to soften at room temperature. In a large bowl combine the Cheddar cheese, cream cheeses, and green onions and mix until well blended. Refrigerate for 20 minutes. Meanwhile, preheat oven to 350° F and toast the pecan halves for 5 to 7 minutes. Remove and let cool. Spoon the cheese mixture onto a decorative serving plate and press the pecans on the outside to adhere. Chill again for at least 1 hour before serving.

 CHILL for 1 hour before serving

 Prep time: 30 minutes

Grilled Chicken Strips with Tangy Peanut Dipping Sauce

Martha might say protect your silver hors d'oeuvres tray from acids with a layer of leafy green lettuce. My thought is, if you're just going to cover up your pretty silver tray, don't bother using it! These are so yummy they'll be gone too quickly to bother!

20 to 30 bamboo skewers
4 to 6 boneless, skinless chicken breasts
1 cup chicken broth
1/2 cup creamy peanut butter
1/8 cup fresh lime juice
1-1/2 Tablespoons firmly packed brown sugar
1 Tablespoon + 1/2 teaspoon soy sauce
1 Tablespoon fresh ginger, peeled & chopped
1 teaspoon fresh cilantro, finely chopped
1/2 teaspoon garlic, minced

In a saucepan over medium-low heat, combine the chicken broth and peanut butter and stir until peanut butter has melted and mixture is smooth. Add in the remaining ingredients and cook for 1 minute more. Remove from heat and chill for 1 hour. Meanwhile, fully immerse the bamboo skewers in water and soak for 30 minutes. Heat the grill. Clean and remove any fat from the chicken and cut into 1 inch wide strips. Spear the chicken onto the skewers and drizzle with some of the sauce. Grill the chicken about 5 minutes per side (be sure not to overcook) and serve warm with the dipping sauce on the side. *Note: No need to soak metal skewers; that's just to ensure the bamboo ones don't catch fire on the grill.*

 CHILL for 1 hour

 Prep time: 10 minutes
Cook time: 10 minutes

Crab Cakes

Martha, I promise this is a good suggestion. Look for the crab <u>claw</u> meat . . . very reasonably priced compared to crab meat.

2 Tablespoons olive oil light
3 Tablespoons yellow onion, chopped
1 stalk celery, chopped
1 container (8 oz.) crab claw meat, drained
1 egg
1 Tablespoon mayonnaise
1 teaspoon spicy mustard
1 cup buttery crackers, crushed
1/4 teaspoon ground cayenne pepper
1 teaspoon garlic, minced
1/4 teaspoon salt
1/2 cup dry bread crumbs
1/3 cup olive oil light

Heat 2 Tablespoons oil in skillet over medium high heat. Sauté onions and celery until tender. In a large bowl, combine crab claw meat, sautéed onions and celery, egg, mayonnaise, mustard, crackers, cayenne pepper, garlic, and salt. Form into 1/2 inch thick patties. Coat the patties with bread crumbs. Heat 1/3 cup oil in same skillet over medium high heat. Cook cakes until golden brown on each side. Drain on paper towel and serve.

Serves: 6

Prep time: 20 minutes
Cook time: 10 - 15 minutes

<u>SAUTÉ</u>: To cook and/or brown food in a small quantity of hot oil or butter.

Cucumber Dip

Cool, refreshing and low in fat.
Serve with Pita bread cut into triangles for dipping.

1 cucumber, peeled
1 cup plain yogurt
1 Tablespoon olive oil
1/2 Tablespoon garlic, minced
1/2 Tablespoon lemon juice
1/8 teaspoon salt

Quarter the cucumber lengthwise and remove all seeds. Thinly slice the quartered cucumber and pat with a paper towel to remove excess water. In a medium bowl, mix the yogurt, olive oil, garlic, lemon juice and salt. Add in the cucumber slices and stir until thoroughly coated. Chill for 2 hours before serving.

Serves: 6

 CHILL for 2 hours

 Prep time: 15 minutes

 CUCUMBER: When shopping for cucumbers, choose long, slender ones for the best quality. They may be dark or medium green, but yellowed ones are undesirable.

Goat Cheese in Red Bell Pepper

A colorful party appetizer sure to be a hit! If you haven't tried Goat Cheese I encourage you to try this as your first taste.

5 oz. goat cheese
3 oz. cream cheese
1 teaspoon garlic, minced
1/3 cup yellow onion, chopped
1 Tablespoon olive oil
1 Tablespoon parsley
1 red bell pepper, short and wide
1 loaf baguette bread, sliced

Mix goat cheese, cream cheese, garlic, onion, oil and parsley together until blended. Cut off top of red bell pepper and remove stem and seeds. Spoon cheese mixture into bell pepper. Place baguette slices into oven and lightly toast. Serve on platter with bell pepper in middle and toasted bread slices garnishing the edges.

Serves: 8 - 10

 Prep time: 15 minutes
Cook time: a few minutes toasting

Guacamole

If you like avocados you will love this recipe. It is outstanding!

3 ripe Hass avocados
1 medium tomato, chopped
1/3 cup red onion, diced
1 Tablespoon lemon juice
2 Tablespoons sour cream
1/2 teaspoon garlic salt
1/8 teaspoon cayenne pepper

In a medium bowl, mash the avocado flesh with a fork. Add tomato, red onion, lemon juice, sour cream, garlic salt, and cayenne pepper. Mix well. Cover and chill until served.
This fresh guacamole is best if served the same day.

Serves: 6

Prep time: 15 minutes

AVOCADO: There are two types found in most grocery stores. Hass avocados have a pebbly, almost black skin. Fuerte, a larger variety, has a smoother, greener skin. Select a heavy avocado with unbroken skin. The fruit should "give" to gentle pressure.

Hummus

Can be made ahead of time.
Serve with warm pita bread cut into triangles for dipping.

1 can (16 oz.) chick peas/garbanzos beans
1/4 cup olive oil
1 Tablespoon lemon juice
1 cup yellow onion, chopped
1 Tablespoon garlic, minced
1 Tablespoon cumin
1/4 teaspoon cayenne pepper
1/2 teaspoon salt

In medium bowl, blend chick peas, olive oil and lemon juice until paste forms. Add onion, garlic, cumin, cayenne pepper and salt. Mix well.

Serves: 10

 Fresh lemon juice will remove onion odor from hands. Or, rub your hands on stainless steel (such as the kitchen sink) to remove food odors.

 Prep time: 10 minutes

Mexican Layered Dip

A hit at pot luck events or casual affairs.

1 can (16.5 oz) refried beans
1 cup sour cream
1-1/2 cups Guacamole (use our entire recipe)
1 cup Salsa (see our recipe)
1/2 cup Cheddar cheese, shredded
2 oz. black olives, pitted and chopped

On a large serving platter, spread refried beans evenly leaving a
border. Spoon sour cream on top, leaving a small border of beans
showing. Repeat with guacamole and salsa so you can see each layer.
Sprinkle the top with cheese and then olives. Serve with tortilla chips.

Serves: 12

 If you brush the grater with oil before you grate cheese, cleanup
will be a snap.

 Prep time: 15 minutes

Stuffed Mushrooms

A great appetizer with a nice bottle of wine!

20 fresh mushrooms, stems removed
1 Tablespoon garlic, minced
1/3 cup Parmesan cheese, grated
1/3 cup yellow onion, finely chopped
1/2 cup bread crumbs
1/2 cup red bell pepper, chopped
1 egg
1 Tablespoon parsley
1/2 teaspoon basil
1/2 teaspoon oregano
1/4 teaspoon salt
1/3 cup melted butter
3/4 cup Mozzarella cheese, shredded

Preheat oven to 350° F. Lightly grease a 9"x13" baking dish. Arrange mushroom caps hollow side up in dish. In medium bowl, mix together garlic, Parmesan cheese, onion, bread crumbs, red bell pepper, egg, parsley, basil, oregano, and salt. Stir in half of the butter until slightly moist. Generously fill mushroom caps with mixture. Sprinkle with Mozzarella cheese. Drizzle remaining butter over filled caps. Bake for 30 minutes until golden.

Serves: 10

 A mushroom's flavor is found in its delicate outer layer. So, if your mushrooms still have some dirt on them, place them in a colander and rinse. Then rub the dirt off gently with your fingers.

 Prep time: 20 minutes
Cook time: 30 minutes

Queso

Martha will love this one. Two no-no's . . . processed cheese and the microwave! It could have been three no-no's, but you can substitute regular Velveeta® instead of Light.

10 oz. Velveeta Cheese Light®, large cubes
1 medium tomato, diced
4 Tablespoons red onion, diced
1 ripe avocado, small cubes

In a medium bowl (microwave safe), combine the cheese, tomatoes, and onions (not the avocado). Heat in microwave for 2 minutes on medium high. Stir with a spoon, and heat for another 2 minutes or until cheese is completely melted. After cooking, add the avocados to the cheese. Serve with tortilla chips or flour tortillas.

Serves: 4

 Prep time: 10 minutes

Shrimp Dip

Surprisingly good and easy. If you really like shrimp you can always add more. Serve with crackers for dipping.

8 oz. cream cheese
1 can (10-3/4 oz.) cream of shrimp soup
1/2 cup cooked salad popcorn shrimp
1 teaspoon garlic, minced
3 Tablespoons of onion, chopped

In a medium bowl, blend cream cheese, soup, shrimp, garlic and onion together. Cover and chill in refrigerator for 2 hours before serving.

Serves: 8

 CHILL for 2 hours

 Prep time: 10 minutes

Lemon Pepper Shrimp

Serve as an appetizer with fresh French bread. Or as a meal with our Alfredo Sauce recipe and pasta.

1/4 cup butter
1/2 Tablespoon garlic, minced
1/4 cup dry white wine (I prefer Chardonnay)
1/2 teaspoon lemon pepper
1 pound fresh shrimp, peeled and deveined

Melt butter in a large skillet over medium heat. Sauté garlic in butter for 1 minute. Pour in wine. Add lemon pepper and shrimp. Cook 3 to 5 minutes until shrimp are pink and tender.

Serves: 4

Prep time: 10 minutes
Cook time: 5 - 7 minutes

Spinach Dip in a Bread Bowl

This dip is tried and true.
If you cannot find a round loaf of bread for the bowl, just serve
the dip in a nice bowl with sliced baguettes on the side.

1 package (10 oz.) frozen chopped spinach,
   thawed and squeezed dry
1-1/2 cups sour cream
1 cup mayonnaise
1 envelope/packet of dried vegetable soup mix
1 can (8 oz.) sliced water chestnuts, drained and diced
3 green onions, finely chopped, white and pale green
   parts only
1 round loaf of bread
(boule, pagnotta, pain au levain or pain de campagne)

In a large bowl, mix together all ingredients, except for the bread, and chill for at least 1 hour or up to a day ahead. To serve, cut a lid from the top of the bread by horizontally slicing about 1-1/2 inches down from the top. Cut or pull out the bread inside the bottom "bowl", leaving about a 1 inch border inside around the crust. Lift bread out carefully and cut or tear into bite size pieces. Fill the empty bread bowl with the chilled dip and serve the bread pieces on the side for dipping.

Serves: 8 - 10

 CHILL for 1 hour before serving

 Prep time: 20 minutes

Tortilla Rollups

A great party pleaser, and you can make it ahead of time.

8 oz. cream cheese, softened
1/2 cup salsa - see our recipe or use your favorite
   brand
10 flour tortillas, fajita size (small)

In a medium bowl, mix cream cheese and salsa together. Spread heaping Tablespoon of mixture evenly on the tortilla. Roll the tortilla. Refrigerate for 1 hour. After chilling, slice into 1 inch long pieces.

Serves: 10 - 15

 You can substitute low fat cream cheese to lighten these.

 CHILL for 1 hour

 Prep time: 15 minutes

Notes

Soups and Salads

Carrot Soup

The bright orange color of this soup makes it perfect for Fall meals. This recipe can be doubled easily.

4 Tablespoons (1/2 stick) unsalted butter
1 medium to large size yellow onion, chopped
14 medium to large size carrots, peeled and sliced
4 cups chicken broth
1/2 cup fresh orange juice

Melt the butter in a stockpot, then add the onion. Sauté until softened. Add the carrot slices and broth. Bring to a boil, then reduce heat and simmer for 20 minutes, until carrot slices are soft. Use a slotted spoon to remove the solids (carrots and onion) to a food processor. Purée to your desired thickness. Return purée back to the pot and bring it to another boil, adding the orange juice. Season to taste with salt and pepper.

Serves: 6 - 8

 Use freshly chopped parsley or chives as an optional garnish.

 Prep time: 25 minutes
Cook time: 25 minutes

Chicken Soup

A hearty lunch dish.

6 cups chicken broth
1 cup baby-cut carrots, chopped
1/2 cup celery, chopped
1/2 cup onion, chopped
2 chicken breasts, skinless and boneless
1/2 cup rice, uncooked

Bring the chicken broth to a boil in a large saucepan over medium heat. Add carrots, celery, and onion. Boil for 15 minutes covered. Reduce heat to low and add chicken breasts and rice. Simmer over low for 20 minutes covered. Carefully remove the chicken breasts, cut into small chunks and return to the pot. Ready to serve.

Serves: 4

 Look closer when buying carrots. Often times, carrot bags have orange lines printed on them. Don't be fooled . . . look carefully.

 Prep time: 10 minutes
Cook time: 35 minutes

Fran's Chili

This chili is not too spicy, so kids love it.

1 pound of lean ground beef (not super lean)
1/2 cup yellow onion, chopped
1 Tablespoon vegetable or canola oil
1 can (28 oz.) crushed tomatoes
1 can (14.5 oz.) diced tomatoes
1 Tablespoon chopped garlic
2 Tablespoons chili powder
1 Tablespoon paprika
1 teaspoon salt
2 cans kidney beans, drained and rinsed

In a large skillet, brown the ground beef with the onion in the oil, then drain off the fat, if necessary. In a large pot, combine the beef and onions with the tomatoes, garlic, chili powder, paprika, and salt. Bring to a boil, then reduce heat to simmer for 1 hour. Add beans and cook for 15 more minutes over medium heat.
This recipe can easily be doubled and is great served over baked potatoes.

Serves: 6

Prep time: 20 minutes
Cook time: 1 hour and 15 minutes

PAPRIKA: A bright red, mild, and sweet pepper, this spice is used in soups, meats, and vegetable dishes. Also commonly used as a garnish for potatoes, salads, and eggs.

French Onion Soup

Incredibly easy and delicious. You will love the reviews!

3 Tablespoons butter
3 medium onions, thinly sliced
1 teaspoon brown sugar
1 Tablespoon all purpose flour
4 cups of beef broth
1 teaspoon Worcestershire sauce
1/2 cup white wine (Chardonnay preferable)
8 slices French bread
1 cup Gruyere cheese, grated

Heat the butter in a large pot over medium heat. Add onions and brown sugar. Cook for 15 minutes until golden. Add the flour; stir for 2 minutes. Add beef broth, Worcestershire sauce, and wine. Cover and simmer for 30 minutes. On a baking sheet, arrange French bread slices. Sprinkle Gruyere cheese on top and toast in oven at 400° F until golden. Serve soup in individual bowls or ramekins with 2 slices of toast on top.

Serves: 4

Prep time: 20 minutes
Cook time: 50 minutes

Chunky Chilled Gazpacho Soup

This soup is great when the temperature rises!

1 can (46 oz.) tomato juice
2 stalks of celery, finely chopped
2 roma tomatoes, finely diced
1 small cucumber, peeled, seeded and finely chopped
1 green onion, finely chopped
1 Tablespoon fresh cilantro, finely chopped
1 Tablespoon lemon juice
2 teaspoons Worcestershire sauce
salt and pepper to taste

Combine all ingredients well and chill. For a smoother soup, purée in a blender or food processor.

Serves: 4

 CHILL to blend flavors

 Try a dollop of light sour cream on top as a garnish.

 Prep time: 15 minutes

Cream of Portabella Mushroom Soup

If you love mushrooms, you will not be able to get enough of this delicious soup!

2 lbs. portabella mushrooms, stems removed
3 small yellow onions
3 Tablespoons unsalted butter
4-1/2 cups water
1-1/2 cups heavy cream
6 Tablespoons medium-dry Sherry

Quarter and thinly slice the mushrooms and chop the onion. In a heavy stockpot, cook mushrooms and onion in butter over moderate heat, stirring occasionally, until softened. Add water and cream; simmer 15 minutes. In a blender, purée half of the mixture. Return purée to the rest of the soup and stir in the Sherry. Add salt and pepper to taste. Warm soup over medium heat until heated through before serving.

Serves: 6

 Use caution when blending hot liquids.

 Prep time: 15 minutes

Baked Potato Soup

A classic that everyone will enjoy.

1/2 cup margarine
1/2 cup all purpose flour
6 cups milk
5 cups peeled and cubed potatoes that have been
   baked
12 green onions, chopped
12 slices cooked bacon, crumbled
1 cup Cheddar cheese, shredded
1 cup sour cream
1 teaspoon salt
1/2 teaspoon ground black pepper

In a large pot, melt margarine over medium heat. Whisk in flour until smooth. Stir in milk, whisking until thickened. Stir in potatoes and onions. Stir frequently and bring to a boil. Reduce heat and simmer for 10 minutes. Mix in bacon, cheese, sour cream, salt, and pepper.

Serves: 6

Prep time: 30 minutes
Cook time: 30 minutes

Tortilla & White Bean Soup

This warm and satisfying soup is especially nice when it's chilly outside.

1 Tablespoon butter or margarine
4 boneless, skinless chicken breast halves, chopped
1 large yellow onion, chopped
3 carrots, chopped
2 garlic cloves, minced
2 cans (14 oz. each) low sodium chicken broth
1 Tablespoon chicken bouillon granules
1 teaspoon ground cumin
3 cans (16 oz. each) Great Northern beans, rinsed, drained, and divided
2 Tablespoons all purpose flour
1/2 cup milk
1/3 cup chopped fresh cilantro
1/3 of a 1-lb. bag white corn tortilla strips

Melt the butter in a large stockpot over medium-high heat. Add chicken and next 3 ingredients, and sauté for 10 minutes. Stir in broth, chicken bouillon granules, and cumin. Bring to a boil. Reduce heat and simmer, stirring occasionally, for 20 minutes. Stir in 2 of the cans of beans. Mash the remaining beans in a small bowl. In a separate bowl, whisk together the flour and milk, and stir into the mashed beans. Gradually add mashed bean mixture to soup, stirring constantly. Cook 10 minutes or until thickened. Remove from heat and stir in the cilantro and tortilla strips.

Serves: 8

 Serve with desired toppings, such as sour cream, shredded Cheddar cheese, sliced green onions, or crumbled bacon.

 Cook time: 40 minutes

Cobb Salad

A great dish for a luncheon. By serving this salad on a large platter your guests can pick exactly which food and how much of each ingredient they want to eat.

1 head romaine lettuce, torn in pieces
Baked Chicken Tenders (use our entire recipe)
4 large hard boiled eggs, diced
8 slices bacon, cooked and crumbled
1 pint cherry tomatoes, cut in half
1/4 cup red onion, diced
1 cup Cheddar cheese, grated
Honey Mustard Dressing (double our recipe)

Spread lettuce on a large serving platter. Arrange Baked Chicken Tenders, eggs, bacon, cherry tomatoes, red onions and Cheddar cheese in separate rows. Serve with Honey Mustard Dressing on the side.

Serves: 8

 Prep time: 1 hour

Ellen's Sensational Salad

Consider substituting ready-to-use lettuce in a bag, which can speed up the prep time without compromising the quality of this sensational salad.

Vinaigrette:
    1/2 cup red wine vinegar
    1/2 cup firmly packed brown sugar
    1/2 cup extra virgin olive oil
    1/8 teaspoon dry mustard

Salad:
    1-1/2 cups pecan pieces
    2 heads of green leaf lettuce or Boston bib
    1-1/2 cans (14 oz. each) hearts of palms, drained & chopped
    1 bunch of fresh parsley, finely chopped
    5 oz. Gorgonzola cheese, crumbled

In a small saucepan, cook the vinegar and brown sugar just until the brown sugar dissolves. Remove from heat and whisk in the olive oil and mustard. Add salt and pepper to taste. Chill before dressing the salad.

Preheat oven to 350° F. Toast the pecan pieces for 5 minutes. Combine all the salad ingredients in a large bowl and toss with the vinaigrette

Serves: 4

 CHILL vinaigrette until cold

 Prep time: 20 minutes
Cook time: 15 minutes

Italian Salad

Martha might slap my hand for the vague title, so please read the list of ingredients.

1 pint cherry tomatoes, quartered
1 cucumber, peeled, sliced thinly
1/3 cup red onion, diced
2 Tablespoons Parmesan cheese, grated
1/3 cup Red Wine Vinaigrette (see our recipe)

In large salad bowl, mix tomatoes, cucumber, red onion, Parmesan cheese, and Vinaigrette Dressing together. Ready to serve.

Serves: 4

 Placing tomatoes in a paper bag at room temperature will help them ripen more quickly. Only store tomatoes in the refrigerator if over ripe.

 Prep time: 10 minutes

Orzo Pasta with Shrimp

A healthy and refreshing pasta salad.

1 can (15 oz.) of corn, drained
1 pound of cooked shrimp, bite size pieces
1/2 cup red onion, chopped
1 cup red bell pepper, chopped
1/2 teaspoon salt
1 teaspoon basil
Ranch Salad Dressing (see our recipe)
1-1/2 cups uncooked orzo

In a large bowl, combine corn, shrimp, red onion, red bell pepper, salt, basil, and our entire recipe of Ranch Salad Dressing. Stir well. Cook the orzo according to package directions and drain. Add orzo to the bowl and toss to blend ingredients completely. Cover and chill until serving.

Serves: 8

 CHILL until serving

 Prep time: 20 minutes
Cook time: 15 minutes

 BASIL: An herb with a sweet, warm flavor and an aromatic odor. Good with fish, roasts, stews, vegetables, and dressings.

Pineapple Chicken Salad

Consider adding a few macadamia nuts to give this a real Hawaiian flavor.

1 box chicken flavored rice & vermicelli mix
1 whole chicken, approximately 3 lbs.
  (or one whole roasted chicken)
3/4 cup mayonnaise
2 teaspoons ground ginger
1 teaspoon salt
1/4 teaspoon ground black pepper
1-1/3 cups diced celery
1 can (20 oz.) pineapple chunks in juice, drained and
  chilled

Prepare rice/vermicelli mixture according to the package directions and let it cool. Boil chicken in water for 45 minutes to 1 hour, then skin and dice. Mix mayonnaise, ginger, salt and pepper in a large bowl. Add celery, pineapple, chicken, and rice. Toss salad. Refrigerate at least 1 hour to let the flavors blend.

CHILL for 1 hour

Prep time: 15 minutes
Cook time: 45 - 60 minutes

Alice's Potato Salad

Martha look away . . . I am suggesting the microwave again.
Winner, winner for a picnic dinner.

5 medium potatoes
5 hard boiled eggs
1 cup mayonnaise
2 teaspoons yellow mustard
1 teaspoon apple cider vinegar
1/4 teaspoon salt
3 sticks of celery, diced

Boil potatoes whole in a large pot of water for 40 minutes. Cool and peel skin off. Cut into 1 inch cubes. Have ready a large bowl and a small bowl. Put the cubed potatoes in the large bowl. Slice boiled eggs in half. Place yolks in the small bowl. Dice egg whites into small pieces and add them to potatoes in the large bowl. In the small bowl, combine mayonnaise, yellow mustard, vinegar, and salt. Mix well and pour over potatoes and eggs. Add celery to mixture in the large bowl and toss completely. For best flavor, chill for an hour before serving.

Serves: 6 - 8

 If time is of the essence, you can microwave the potatoes instead of boiling them. Just set the microwave on high for 13 to 15 minutes and they are cooked.

 CHILL for 1 hour before serving

 Prep time: 25 minutes
Cook time: 40 minutes

Taco Salad

Feel free to add or delete ingredients to your liking. ¡Olé!

1 lb. ground beef or turkey
1 packet (1.5 oz.) of taco seasoning
1/3 of a 15 oz. bag Fritos® corn chips
2 heads of green leaf lettuce, torn to bite size pieces
3 medium tomatoes, chopped large
1 can (16 oz.) kidney beans, drained and rinsed
2 cups (approx.) jicama, peeled and chopped
1/2 cup (approx.) Cheddar cheese, finely shredded
Catalina salad dressing
2-3 avocados, cut into large chunks

Brown the ground beef or turkey in a large skillet. Drain off the fat, then add the packet of taco seasoning and the water (according to the packet directions) and cook until most of the liquid has evaporated. Place the corn chips in a large bowl, top with the cooked meat, and place in the fridge to cool. In a large salad bowl, add the lettuce, tomatoes, kidney beans, jicama, and cheese. Toss with as much or as little dressing as you like. Add the beef and corn chips mixture, and toss again. Add the avocados last, just before serving.

Serves: 5 - 6 people as a main dish, and can be doubled easily

 CHILL before tossing to serve

 Prep time: 10 minutes
Cook time: 15 minutes

Tortellini Pasta Salad

Give your pasta salad a little zip!

19 oz. cheese-filled tortellini
1 red bell pepper, chopped
1 can (6 oz.) black olives, pitted and sliced
4 oz. feta cheese, crumbed
1/4 teaspoon salt
Creamy Italian Vinaigrette (see our recipe)

In large pot of boiling water, cook tortellini until al dente. Drain and rinse. In a large bowl, combine tortellini, red bell pepper, black olives, feta cheese, and salt. Add entire recipe of Creamy Italian Dressing and toss.

Serves: 8

 Prep time: 20 minutes
Cook time: 15 minutes

 AL DENTE: Pasta cooked until tender, but with some firmness.

Tuna Salad

*Serve over a slice of Beefsteak tomato or on a bed of lettuce.
I make it with Miracle Whip Light®, but you can substitute
mayonnaise if you like.*

2 cans (6 oz. each) albacore tuna
1 granny smith apple, diced
1/4 cup red onion, diced
1/2 cup Miracle Whip Light®

In a medium bowl, mix all ingredients together. That's it . . . salad is
ready to serve!

Serves: 4

When buying canned tuna, do not assume that water versus oil in
the can lowers the fat content. The amount of fat in tuna varies
with when and where it was caught. So, be sure to check the
label for fat grams.

Prep time: 10 minutes

Wild Rice and Chicken Salad

Unlike most chicken salad recipes, this one uses yogurt instead of mayonnaise.

1 box white & wild long grain rice
1 cup walnut pieces
2 cups cooked chicken, shredded or cubed
1 cup diced celery
1/3 cup finely chopped green onion
  (white & pale green parts only)
6 oz. plain yogurt
1/4 teaspoon lemon zest
2 Tablespoons lemon juice
2 Tablespoons extra virgin olive oil

Cook the rice according to the package directions then remove from heat. Toast the walnut pieces at 350° F for 5 minutes. In a large bowl, combine the yogurt, lemon zest, juice, olive oil, salt and pepper to taste. Add the chicken, celery, and green onion. Finally, add the cooled walnuts and 1-1/2 cups of the cooked rice (you will have rice left over for another use). Mix all ingredients together well and chill for at least 1 hour.

When selecting lemons, choose those heavy for their size. Smoother, thinner skins usually indicate more juice. Most skin markings do not affect quality. Light or greenish-yellow lemons are more tart than deep yellow ones. Avoid fruits showing withered, sunken, soft areas, or mold.

CHILL for 1 hour before serving

Prep time: 35 minutes
Cook time: 25 minutes

Blue Cheese Dressing

A favorite! Try with a wedge of iceberg lettuce, diced red onions and diced tomatoes.

1 cup sour cream
1/2 cup mayonnaise
1 teaspoon Worcestershire sauce
1 teaspoon lemon juice
1/4 teaspoon salt
1/4 teaspoon ground black pepper
4 ounces blue cheese, crumbled

In a medium bowl, whisk together sour cream, mayonnaise, Worcestershire sauce, lemon juice, salt and pepper. Stir in blue cheese. Cover and refrigerate 30 minutes before serving.

Serves: 12

 CHILL for 30 minutes

 Prep time: 10 minutes

 BLUE CHEESE (France): A white, semi-soft cheese with blue-green veins. Spicy and piquant, it keeps 3 to 8 months. Used in salads and dips.

Creamy Italian Vinaigrette

3/4 cup mayonnaise
1-1/2 Tablespoons red wine vinegar
1/2 Tablespoon lemon juice
3 Tablespoons olive oil light
1 teaspoon Worcestershire sauce
1/2 teaspoon dried oregano
1 teaspoon granulated sugar
1 teaspoon garlic, minced

In medium bowl, whisk together mayonnaise, red wine vinegar, lemon juice, olive oil, Worcestershire sauce, oregano, sugar and garlic. Cover and refrigerate for 30 minutes before serving.

 CHILL for 30 minutes

 Prep time: 10 minutes

Lemony Caesar Salad Dressing

Best served over romaine lettuce with garlicky croutons.

1/2 cup Parmesan cheese, grated
1/3 cup extra virgin olive oil
1/3 cup vegetable (or canola or safflower) oil
1/3 cup fresh lemon juice
2 teaspoons garlic cloves, chopped
1 teaspoon Worcestershire sauce
Dash of salt & freshly ground black pepper

Combine all ingredients in a blender or mini food processor and blend until well combined. Can be made up to a day ahead and chilled.

 Prep time: 10 minutes

Tangy Spinach Salad Dressing

1/2 cup vegetable oil (or use olive, canola, or
    safflower oil instead)
1/3 cup yellow onion, chopped
1/4 cup packed brown sugar
1/4 cup red wine vinegar
2 Tablespoons ketchup
1 teaspoon Worcestershire sauce
1 teaspoon dry mustard

Combine all ingredients in a blender or mini food processor and blend until well combined. Can be made up to a day ahead and chilled. Best served over spinach with sliced hard-boiled eggs, crumbled bits of bacon, croutons, mandarin orange segments and cherry tomatoes.

 Prep time: 10 minutes

Honey Mustard Dressing

Can be low fat by using light mayonnaise. Use as a dip for our Chicken Tenders or as a dressing for our Cobb Salad.

1/4 cup mayonnaise
1 Tablespoon honey
1 Tablespoon yellow mustard
1 teaspoon lemon juice

In a small bowl, whisk together mayonnaise, honey, mustard, and lemon juice. Store in the refrigerator covered until ready to use.

 Prep time: 5 minutes

Ranch Dressing

1/2 cup mayonnaise
1/2 cup sour cream
1 teaspoon dried chives
1/2 teaspoon dried parsley
1/2 teaspoon oregano
1/2 teaspoon dried dill weed
1/8 teaspoon garlic salt
2 teaspoons onion, minced
1/2 teaspoon Worcestershire sauce
1/8 teaspoon ground black pepper

In a medium bowl, whisk together all ingredients. Cover and refrigerate for 30 minutes before serving.

Serves: 8

 CHILL for 30 minutes

 Prep time: 10 minutes
Serve time: 30 minutes

 DILL: This herb may be used to garnish or cook with fish, soup, dressings, potatoes and beans.

Red Wine Vinaigrette

The perfect dressing for our Italian Salad recipe.

> 2 Tablespoons red wine vinegar
> 1/2 teaspoon lemon juice
> 1/8 teaspoon salt
> 1/8 teaspoon pepper
> 1/4 cup olive oil

In a medium bowl, mix the red wine vinegar, lemon juice, salt, and pepper. Add the olive oil slowly while beating with a whisk until mixture emulsifies.

Serves: 4

 Do not use a metal bowl when mixing salads. Wooden, glass, or ceramic bowls are recommended.

 Prep time: 5 minutes

 EMULSIFY: To convert two or more liquids from an oily substance to a fluid, giving it the resemblance of a blended solution.

Notes

Vegetables, Side Dishes, and Sauces

Oven Roasted Asparagus

Try this flavorful alternative instead of steaming.

1 lb. bunch (approx.) asparagus
2 Tablespoons extra virgin olive oil
2 Tablespoons freshly minced thyme

Preheat oven to 450° F and line a baking sheet with foil. Trim tough ends off the asparagus and place in a rectangular bowl or dish. Add the olive oil, thyme, salt and pepper to taste. Toss to coat the asparagus. Arrange the asparagus in a single layer on the lined baking sheet. Roast in the oven, uncovered, for 7 to 10 minutes, or until softened but still bright green.
Roasted asparagus is also good drizzled with a little balsamic vinegar.

Serves: 4

Prep time: 10 minutes
Cook time: 10 minutes

SAUVIGNON BLANC also goes well with:
Cheese: Feta, Chevre
Meat: chicken, turkey
Seafood: sole, oysters, scallops
Veggies: asparagus

Broccoli Soufflé

An impressive dish for your special guests. If you follow the directions carefully the results are almost guaranteed!

3 Tablespoons butter, plus some for coating pan
4 Tablespoons all purpose flour
1-1/2 cups milk
6 egg yolks
1-1/4 cups broccoli florets, cooked and chopped
1 Tablespoon onion, chopped
5 Tablespoons Parmesan cheese, grated
1/8 teaspoon pepper
8 egg whites
1/8 teaspoon salt
1/8 teaspoon cream of tarter

Preheat oven to 350° F. In a medium saucepan, melt butter. Whisk in the flour, stirring until smooth. Add milk and whisk over medium-low heat until thickened. Remove from the burner and add egg yolks, broccoli, onion, Parmesan cheese, and pepper. Mix thoroughly. In a medium bowl, add egg whites, salt, and cream of tarter. Whisk egg whites until they are stiff. Add a few Tablespoons of the egg whites to the broccoli mixture. Butter a 6-cup soufflé dish. Fold the broccoli mixture (see below) into the soufflé dish. Bake the soufflé in the center of the oven for 35 to 40 minutes. Serve at once.

Serves: 6

Prep time: 30 minutes
Cook time: 35 - 40 minutes

FOLD: To gently combine one ingredient with another by using two motions, cutting vertically through the mixture with a spoon or spatula and gently turning the ingredients over on top of each other, and rotating the bowl 1/4 turn with each stroke. The term is often used in instructions relating to beaten egg whites.

Rena's Tahiti Carrots

This dish was inspired by a trip to the islands of the South Pacific.

1 lb. fresh baby-cut carrots (or regular carrots, cut into rounds)
1 cup mango juice or nectar
2 Tablespoons unsalted butter
1/4 teaspoon granulated sugar
1/3 teaspoon ground cinnamon

Place the carrots in a medium saucepan and add just enough water to cover them (about 2 cups). Bring water to a boil, then reduce heat to medium-low and continue to cook for 10 minutes. Reserve 1/3 cup of the cooking water from the pot, then drain the carrots and set aside. In a blender, combine the 1/3 cup of water, 1 cup mango juice, and 1/2 cup of the carrots. Puree this mixture, then return it to the pot and boil, uncovered, for approximately 10 minutes. The mixture should reduce down to 3/4 cup. (*If this reduces to less, just add enough additional mango juice until you have 3/4 cup.*) Turn heat down to a low simmer and stir in the remaining ingredients. Season to taste with salt and pepper. Add the cooked carrots back into the pot and stir well to coat and heat through.

Serves: 6

 Cook time: 25 minutes

Broiled Portabella Mushrooms with Pesto and Goat Cheese

These are very flavorful and great as an appetizer or side dish.

4 portabella mushroom caps, stems removed
4 Tablespoons extra virgin olive oil
1/2 cup prepared pesto sauce (see Premo Pesto Sauce
   recipe or use purchased)
1 large roma tomato, diced
4 Tablespoons mild goat cheese
2 Tablespoons balsamic vinegar

Preheat oven to 400° F and line a baking sheet with foil. Place the mushroom caps, skin side down, and drizzle each with a Tablespoon of olive oil, then salt and pepper them to taste. Bake for 15 minutes, or until soft. Remove from the oven and change the temperature setting to Broil. Next, spread the pesto sauce evenly over the mushrooms and top with the diced tomato. Crumble 1 Tablespoon of goat cheese over each cap. (This recipe *can be done several hours ahead to this point.*) Broil just until goat cheese begins to color, about 2 to 3 minutes. Drizzle with balsamic vinegar and serve.
This recipe can easily be doubled.

Serves: 4

Prep time: 10 minutes
Cook time: 15 - 18 minutes

Creamed Spinach

An all time favorite dish of "Popeye the Sailor".

1 Tablespoon butter
1 cup onion, chopped
20 oz. fresh spinach, tough stems removed
1/4 cup cream cheese
1 Tablespoon half and half
1/2 teaspoon oregano
1/4 teaspoon salt
1/4 teaspoon pepper

Preheat oven to 375° F. In a large sauté pan, melt butter over medium heat. Add onion and sauté for 3 minutes. Add spinach and cover. Cook until spinach wilts, approximately 2 minutes. Add cream cheese, half and half, oregano, salt and pepper. Cook another minute uncovered until cheese melts. Spoon mixture into a small casserole dish. Bake for 30 minutes.

Serves: 4

Prep time: 15 minutes
Cook time: 35 minutes

SPINACH: When shopping, select emerald-green spinach with crisp but tender leaves and slender stems. Squeeze the bag – spinach leaves should feel springy. When preparing spinach, strip the coarse stems from curly-leaf variety. You can leave the stems flat-leaf spinach.

Zucchini

An easy side dish that melts in your mouth.

> 2 zucchini
> 3 Tablespoons butter
> 1/2 cup Parmesan cheese, grated

Preheat oven to 400° F. Slice zucchini lengthwise, yielding 4 slices per zucchini. Butter one side of each zucchini slice evenly and place top up on foil covered cookie sheet. Sprinkle Parmesan cheese evenly on all buttered zucchini. Bake for 20-25 minutes until golden on top.

Serves: 4

Prep time: 5 minutes
Cook time: 20 - 25 minutes

Beer Baked Beans

Martha, I never claimed to be a classy chick.
Beans are better with beer!

4 slices bacon, cut into 1" pieces
1 cup red onion, chopped
2 cans (15 oz.) pinto beans, drained and rinsed
1 can (8 oz.) tomato sauce
1/2 cup beer (leaded or non-leaded)
3/4 cup firmly packed brown sugar
1 teaspoon Worcestershire sauce

Preheat oven to 350° F. In a medium pan, sauté the bacon and onions over medium heat. Cook until onions are soft, about 10 minutes. In a 2 quart dish, combine the bacon and onion mixture, drained pinto beans, tomato sauce, beer, brown sugar, and Worcestershire sauce. Bake uncovered for 30 minutes.

Serves: 8

Prep time: 10 minutes
Cook time: 40 minutes

BEANS: Available in several varieties, beans provide substantial amounts of fiber. Thus, beans help prevent colon cancer, heart disease, and stroke.

Black Bean Patties

A nice compliment to any grilled fish or chicken entrée.
Surprisingly tasty!

1 can (15 oz.) black beans, drained and rinsed
1/3 cup onion, diced
1 teaspoon garlic salt
1/4 teaspoon cayenne pepper
5 Tablespoons all purpose flour
1/4 cup oil
1/2 cup sour cream

In a medium bowl, mash black beans to form a paste. Add onion, garlic salt, cayenne pepper, and flour to the bowl and mix together. In a large frying pan, heat oil over medium high heat. Scoop the bean mixture by heaping Tablespoon into the hot oil, forming 2 inch patties. Cook the patties for 4 minutes on each side. Serve with sour cream on top.

Serves: 4

 Prep time: 15 minutes
Cook time: 8 minutes

Deviled Eggs

Hey Martha look . . . no paprika!

1 dozen large eggs
1 cup mayonnaise
2 teaspoon yellow mustard
1 teaspoon apple cider vinegar

Put the eggs in large pot and fill with cold water covering the eggs by one inch. Bring water to a boil and then turn off heat. Cover pot and leave on burner for 20 minutes. Remove pot and rinse eggs under cool water until room temperature. Peel the eggs, rinse, and cut each in half lengthwise. Remove yolks and place in a medium bowl. Set aside the egg white halves. Crush yolks with a fork. Mix in mayonnaise, mustard, and vinegar. Scoop heaping teaspoon of mixture to fill each egg white half. Chill for 1 hour before serving.

Yields: 24 halves

 CHILL for 1 hour

 Prep time: 10 minutes
Cook time: 20 minutes

Eggplant Parmesan

*If you like the taste of eggplant, you will enjoy this recipe.
Serve over buttered pasta and it makes a great meal.*

2 eggs
1 cup plain bread crumbs
1 Tablespoon parsley
1/2 Tablespoon oregano
1 Tablespoon garlic salt
1 eggplant, peeled, sliced lengthwise (1/2" thick)
1 can (14.5 oz.) Italian style diced tomatoes
1 cup Mozzarella cheese, shredded
1/4 cup Parmesan cheese, grated

Preheat oven to 400° F. In a medium bowl, beat the eggs. In another
bowl, mix bread crumbs, parsley, oregano, and garlic salt. Dip
eggplant slices in egg and then in bread crumbs covering both sides.
Place coated slices in a 9" x 13" baking dish. Cover the dish with foil
and bake for 20 minutes. Remove from oven and add diced tomatoes
evenly on top. Sprinkle Mozzarella and Parmesan cheese over the
eggplant. Return to oven, uncovered, for 20 minutes. Bake until
golden.

Serves: 4

Prep time: 20 minutes
Cook time: 40 minutes

Macaroni & Cheese

A kid friendly meal or a great side dish for a picnic.

3 Tablespoons butter
2 Tablespoons all purpose flour
1-3/4 cups milk
1-1/2 cups Cheddar cheese, shredded
1/4 teaspoon salt
8 oz. small shell pasta, cooked

Preheat oven to 350° F. Melt butter in a medium saucepan over medium heat. Add the flour and whisk rapidly. Stir in milk and cook until thick, 5 minutes or so. Add the cheese and salt. Stir until completely melted. Pour the cheese mixture into a 2 quart casserole dish. Add cooked macaroni to dish and mix evenly. Bake for 15 minutes.

Serves: 4

Be sure to cool this dish a bit before serving to children.

Prep time: 15 minutes
Cook time: 15 minutes

Parmesan-Basil Polenta

Try this instead of mashed potatoes as an alternative side dish.

5 cups water
1-1/2 cups coarse cornmeal
1/2 teaspoon salt
1/2 cup Parmesan cheese, grated
1 Tablespoon fresh basil, chopped
2 cloves garlic, minced
1/4 cup extra virgin olive oil

Bring water to a boil in a medium saucepan. Whisk in the cornmeal and continue stirring until smooth. Turn the heat down to simmer and add the salt. Stir often and cook for 10 minutes. Add remaining ingredients, remove from heat, and serve.

Serves: 8

 Leftover polenta can be spooned into a pan and chilled overnight. When ready to serve, cut into wedges or squares and grill until heated through.

 Prep time: 5 minutes
Cook time: 15 minutes

Au Gratin Potatoes

A fabulous side dish for any meat entree.

4 potatoes, peeled and sliced into 1/8" slices
1/4 cup onion, chopped
2 Tablespoons butter
2 Tablespoons all purpose flour
1-3/4 cups milk
1 teaspoon salt
1-1/4 cups Cheddar cheese, shredded

Preheat oven to 400° F. Butter a 9" x 13" casserole dish. Layer the potatoes into bottom of casserole dish. Top with onions. In a medium saucepan, melt butter over medium heat. Add flour and whisk. Stir in milk and add salt. Heat until thickened, stirring constantly for several minutes. Add cheese and blend the mixture while cheese melts. Pour mixture over the potatoes. Cover with aluminum foil and bake for 1 hour and 15 minutes.

Serves: 4

Prep time: 30 minutes
Cook time: 1 hour 15 minutes

AU GRATIN: Topped with cheese and/or crumbs. Browned in the oven or under the broiler.

Herbed Home Fried Potatoes

A great side for breakfast or dinner.

4 lbs. red new potatoes
3 cups yellow onion, finely chopped
1/2 cup extra virgin olive oil
1 teaspoon dried rosemary, crushed or crumbled
1/4 cup fresh parsley, finely chopped

Boil potatoes until they are just tender (about 6 to 10 minutes, depending on the size of the potatoes). Drain and let cool. Once cool, cut into approximately 1" chunks and place them in a large bowl. Add the onion, 2 Tablespoons of olive oil, rosemary, parsley, salt and pepper to taste. Mix well.
Note: Recipe can be done several hours or up to 1 day ahead to this point.
Meanwhile, heat 3 Tablespoons of olive oil in a large skillet until hot, but not smoking. Working in batches, add some of the potato mixture to the pan and sauté over medium-high heat, stirring for 10 to 15 minutes, or until the potatoes are golden. Transfer to a serving dish and cover with foil to keep warm. Repeat with the remaining oil and potatoes until all are cooked.

Serves: 8

 If serving these for breakfast or brunch, prepare the potatoes the night before so all you will have to do is sauté them in the morning.

 Prep time: 10 minutes
Cook time: 25 minutes

Mashed Potatoes with Leeks

The best mashed potatoes are light and lump-free.

> 4 Tablespoons (1/2 stick) unsalted butter, divided
> 1 medium size leek, white and light green parts only
> 2 large (or 3 small) russet potatoes
> 1/3 cup half and half

Rinse the leek well, running water through the layers to remove sand, then chop it finely (you should have approximately 3/4 cup). Sauté the leek in 2 Tablespoons butter over low heat until translucent (do not brown) and set aside. Peel the potatoes then cut into even size chunks. Boil the potatoes until soft, approximately 15 to 20 minutes. Drain and mash the potatoes in a large bowl. Add the leek, the rest of the butter and the half and half. Mash until smooth and add salt and pepper to taste.

Serves: 4

Prep time: 10 minutes
Cook time: 20 minutes

LEEKS: Resemble a very large green onion. The thinner leeks are the more tender. Cut off the dark green tops, then trim roots, split stems lengthwise and rinse thoroughly. Often, soil is trapped in the base of the layers.

JoAnna's Parmesan Potato Wedges

This recipe appeals to the kid in me with a touch of sophistication.

4 medium russet potatoes
1/2 cup olive oil light
1/2 cup Parmesan cheese, grated
1/4 teaspoon garlic salt

Preheat oven to 375° F. Leave skins on potatoes and cut them into wedges (8 wedges per potato). In a 9" x 13" casserole dish, arrange slices in 2 rows lengthwise. Pour oil over potatoes evenly. Sprinkle Parmesan cheese and garlic salt on top evenly. Bake, uncovered, for 30 minutes.

Serves: 4

 When cooking in glass dishes, reduce oven temperature by 25 degrees.

 Prep time: 10 minutes
Cook time: 30 minutes

Twice Baked Potatoes

You can always use a microwave to initially bake the potatoes. However, Martha wouldn't like that!

4 small to medium sized potatoes
3 Tablespoons butter
1/2 cup milk
1/2 cup cream cheese
1/2 cup Cheddar cheese, shredded
1/2 cup half and half
1 teaspoon salt
1/4 teaspoon pepper

Heat oven to 425° F. Wrap each potato in aluminum foil and bake until softened, about 1 hour. Let the potatoes cool, and lower oven temperature to 350° F. Cut the potatoes in half lengthwise. Carefully scoop out potato flesh, not breaking the skins. Blend together the potatoes, butter, milk, cream cheese, Cheddar cheese, half and half, salt, and pepper. Scoop the mixture into the reserved skins and arrange on a baking sheet. Bake for 15 minutes until golden.

Serves: 4

 Occasionally, I destroy the potato skin by accident. If you do so, just discard the skin and put the mixture into a casserole dish. Now call them Cheesy Potato Casserole.

 Prep time: 15 minutes
Cook time: 1 hour 15 minutes

 CABERNET SAUVIGNON also goes well with:
Cheese: Cheddar
Meat: beef
Veggies: caramelized onions
Other: chocolate

Fried Rice

A great side dish for any grilled meat.

1-2/3 cups water
1-1/2 cups uncooked white rice (yields 4 cups cooked)
1/2 teaspoon lemon juice
4 teaspoons olive oil light
3 eggs, lightly beaten
1 cup green peas, cooked
6 green onions, chopped, yielding ¼ cup
1 can (5 oz.) drained water chestnuts, sliced
2 Tablespoons soy sauce
1/8 teaspoon ground ginger

In a medium saucepan, bring water to boil. Stir in rice and lemon juice. Reduce heat to low, cover and simmer for 20 minutes. In a large frying pan heat 1 teaspoon of oil and tilt to coat pan evenly. Add eggs and cook for 3 minutes. Flip eggs and cook for 1 more minute. Remove and cut into thin slices and set aside. Heat 3 teaspoons of oil in same frying pan over medium high heat. Add peas, onions, and water chestnuts. Cook for 3 minutes, tossing constantly. Mix in soy sauce and ginger to pan. Stir in rice and eggs, and heat for 1 more minute. Ready to serve.

Serves: 4

 Adding a teaspoon of lemon juice to each quart (4 cups) of water used to cook rice will ensure the grains stay white and separated.

 Prep time: 15 minutes
Cook time: 30 minutes

Lemon Rice with Almonds

This is a nice alternative to plain white rice as a side dish.

1 Tablespoon unsalted butter
3 Tablespoons minced yellow onion
1/2 cup long grain white rice
1 cup chicken broth
zest of 1 small lemon
2 Tablespoons lemon juice
1/4 cup slivered almonds

Melt the butter in a saucepan over medium heat. Add the onion and sauté for 1 minute. Add the rice and stir for 2 minutes. Add the broth, zest, and lemon juice and bring to a boil, then reduce heat, cover, and simmer for 20 minutes. Meanwhile, toast the almonds at 350° F for 3 to 5 minutes. When the rice is done, stir in the almonds and serve.

Serves: 2

Prep time: 10 minutes
Cook time: 25 minutes

ZEST: The outer-most part of the rind of an orange or lemon, grated just down to the white pith underneath. Synonymous with minced orange or lemon peel.

Wild Rice and Sausage Casserole

This side dish goes great with chicken, pork, or beef dishes.

1 box Uncle Ben's® (or other brand) white & wild rice
1 lb. tube sausage
1 cup yellow onion, diced
8 oz. sliced mushrooms
1 cup whole milk
1/4 cup flour
1 cup chicken broth
1/4 cup (1/2 stick) unsalted butter, melted
1/4 teaspoon dried thyme

Cook the rice according to the package directions and set aside in a large bowl. Meanwhile, stir the sausage and the onion in a large skillet over medium heat. When the sausage is just about halfway cooked, add the mushrooms and sauté until sausage is cooked through. Remove from heat and add to the bowl containing rice. Spray a deep casserole dish with cooking spray and preheat oven to 350° F. In a smaller bowl, whisk together the milk and flour until smooth, then add the remaining ingredients. Season to taste with salt and pepper and pour over the sausage and rice. Stir well and spoon into the prepared casserole dish. Bake, uncovered, for 30 minutes.

Serves: 6 - 8

 When preparing your favorite casserole, make it in 2 smaller pans and freeze one for a busy day.

 Prep time: 20 minutes
Cook time: 15 minutes

Creamy Tomato Risotto

Fair warning: This side dish takes approximately 25 minutes to prepare and MUST be stirred constantly. Otherwise, it's very easy and well worth the elbow grease.

1-1/2 Tablespoons extra virgin olive oil
3/4 cup yellow onion, diced
1 cup risotto rice (a.k.a. arborio rice)
4 cups low salt chicken broth, heated
3/4 cup canned diced plum tomatoes with juice
2 teaspoons fresh rosemary, finely chopped
1/2 cup Parmesan cheese, grated

In a stock pot, heat the oil over medium heat and sauté the onion until softened. Stir in the rice and cook for 3 minutes. Reduce heat to medium-low and add 1 cup of the hot chicken broth. Stir constantly at a simmer until the rice has absorbed the broth. Repeat, adding 1/2 cup of the broth at a time and continue until just 1/2 cup of the broth remains. Add the tomatoes, rosemary, salt and pepper to taste. Add remaining broth 1/4 cup at a time until all is well absorbed and risotto is creamy in texture. Remove from heat and gently stir in the Parmesan cheese.

Serves: 4 - 6

 Cook time: 25 minutes

Tomato and Zucchini Tart

You can use your favorite pie crust recipe,
or do as I recommend: use a prepared crust to save time.
I'll bet Martha would never suggest that!

1 refrigerated 8" or 9" pie crust
2 to 3 roma tomatoes
1 medium zucchini
25 to 30 fresh basil leaves, large and small
4 Tablespoons extra virgin olive oil
1 clove garlic, minced
1/3 cup Gruyere (or Swiss) cheese, grated

Bake the piecrust according to the package directions until it is just golden. Take the crust out and adjust the oven temperature to 350° F. Meanwhile, slice the zucchini and tomatoes into 1/8 inch thick slices. Chop about 10 of the smaller basil leaves and add to a small bowl with the olive oil, garlic, salt and pepper to taste. Spread the cheese evenly on the bottom of the baked piecrust. Arrange the remaining basil leaves on top of the cheese. Brush each slice of tomato and zucchini with the basil-garlic oil mixture. Arrange the tomato and zucchini slices alternately, overlapping slightly, in a single layer over the basil leaves in the pie shell. Bake until the vegetables are warm and tender, about 10 to 15 minutes. Best served warm.

Serves: 8

 Since this crust is baked twice, it's a good idea to cover the edge of the crust with foil before the second baking to avoid burning it.

 Prep time: 20 minutes
Cook time: 10 - 15 minutes

Light Alfredo Sauce

*Tastes just as good as traditional Alfredo Sauce but not as heavy.
Serve with any type of pasta.*

4 Tablespoons butter
1 Tablespoon all purpose flour
1 cup half and half
1 teaspoon garlic, minced
1 cup Parmesan cheese, grated

Melt butter in a medium saucepan over medium low heat. Add flour
and whisk the mixture for 30 seconds. Add half and half and heat for 5
minutes. Add the garlic and Parmesan cheese, and whisk quickly to
blend the sauce.

Serves: 4

 Traditional Alfredo Sauce recipes call for twice the amount of
butter and heavy cream instead of half and half.

 Cook time: 10 minutes

Avocado & Corn Salsa

This could also be labeled a "chutney" or "salad", but whatever you prefer to call it, I'm sure it will soon be one of your favorites.

2 cans (15-1/4 oz.) whole kernel corn, drained
1-1/2 cups red cherry tomatoes, quartered
1/2 cup red onion, diced
1 Tablespoon fresh lemon juice
1 Tablespoon chili powder
2 teaspoons ground cumin
1 teaspoon rice vinegar
1/8 teaspoon cayenne pepper
1/8 teaspoon garlic salt
1/2 cup (1/2 bunch) fresh cilantro, stemmed & chopped
2 avocados (ripe but slightly firm), diced

Combine all ingredients except the cilantro and avocado. Mix well. *Note: You can prepare the salsa up to this point one day before serving.* Just before serving, add the cilantro and avocado and toss gently.

 This salsa is great along side burgers, or as a topping to tacos.

 Prep time: 10 minutes

Easy Hollandaise Sauce

This sauce is a must for Eggs Benedict and is also great over steamed asparagus.

3 large egg yolks
1-1/2 Tablespoons lemon juice
1/4 teaspoon salt
1 teaspoon freshly chopped chives or parsley
 (or 1/2 teaspoon dried)
dash of white pepper
1/2 cup (1 stick) unsalted butter, melted and very hot

Combine egg yolks, lemon juice, salt, chives and pepper in a blender. Cover and blend at high speed for about 15 seconds. Pour in about 1/3 of the melted butter and blend again. Repeat until all the butter has been blended and the sauce is creamy.

Yields: 3/4 cup

To make Eggs Benedict, toast an English muffin and top it with a slice of hot ham or Canadian bacon, a poached egg, and Hollandaise sauce.

Serve time: 10 minutes

Orange Cranberry Sauce

This is a must for Thanksgiving dinner and is also wonderful in Margo's Cranberry Chicken.

1-1/4 cups frozen cranberry juice concentrate, thawed
1/3 cup granulated sugar
1 package (12 oz.) fresh cranberries, rinsed & drained
1/2 cup dried cranberries (about 2 oz.)
3 Tablespoons orange marmalade
2 Tablespoons fresh orange juice
2 teaspoons orange zest
1/4 teaspoon ground allspice

Combine cranberry juice concentrate and sugar in heavy medium saucepan. Bring to boil over high heat, stirring until sugar dissolves. Add fresh and dried cranberries. Cook mixture until the dried berries begin to soften and fresh berries begin to pop, stirring often, about 7 minutes. Remove from heat and stir in orange marmalade, orange juice, zest, and allspice. Cool completely. Cover, and chill for 2 hours. *Can be made up to 3 days ahead. Keep refrigerated.*

Yields: 2-1/2 cups

 CHILL for 2 hours

 Prep time: 10 minutes
Cook time: 15 minutes

Premo Pesto Sauce

There are several variations of pesto sauces, but this is a good one to start with.

1/3 cup pine nuts (or walnuts)
1-1/4 cups fresh basil leaves
1/2 cup Parmesan cheese, grated
1/2 cup extra virgin olive oil
2 garlic cloves, peeled & chopped

Preheat oven to 350° F. Toast the pine nuts for about 5 minutes, or until they are just golden. Set aside and let cool. Meanwhile, combine all the remaining ingredients in a small food processor or blender. Turn the machine on and off rapidly, pulsing the ingredients together until coarsely chopped. Season with just a bit of salt and pepper and add the pine nuts. Blend until sauce is just a bit more smooth.
This sauce is great on homemade pizza, pasta, grilled salmon, or as an appetizer dipping sauce.

Yields: 1 cup

Prep time: 20 minutes
Cook time: 15 minutes

Salsa

Texas style. Serve with tortilla chips or use in our Tortilla Rollups and Mexican Layered Dip recipes.

1-1/2 cups fresh tomatoes
3/4 cup onion
2 Tablespoons jalapeno peppers (2 peppers)
1 Tablespoon lime juice (1 large lime)
3 Tablespoons cilantro leaves (1 bunch)

Place tomatoes, onion, jalepeno peppers, lime juice, and cilantro in a blender or food processor. Blend on low to desired consistency.

Yields: 2-1/2 cups

 To avoid tears when cutting onions, try cutting them under cold running water or placing them in the freezer briefly before cutting.

 Prep time: 15 minutes

Notes

Entrees and Main Dishes

"BBQ" Meat Loaf

Don't let the name fool you – no grill is necessary!

1 small to medium size yellow onion, chopped
1-1/2 pounds of lean ground beef (not super lean)
1/2 cup Italian (or plain) bread crumbs
1 egg, beaten
1 teaspoon salt
1/4 teaspoon black pepper
2 cans (8 oz. each) tomato sauce (plain)
1/2 cup water
3 Tablespoons vinegar (white or cider)
3 Tablespoons brown sugar
2 Tablespoons Dijon mustard
2 teaspoons Worcestershire sauce

Sauté the onion in a saucepan over medium heat until just soft, then remove from heat. Preheat the oven to 350° F. In a large bowl, mix the beef, bread crumbs, egg, salt, pepper, and half of one of the cans of tomato sauce together. Form the mixture into a loaf and place in a deep baking dish sprayed with cooking spray. In a small bowl, combine the rest of the tomato sauce and all other ingredients, mixing well. Pour the sauce mixture over the loaf and bake, uncovered, for 1 hour and 15 minutes. Baste the meat with the sauce occasionally.

Serves: 6

Best served with a bit of the extra sauce from the baking dish spooned over steamed white rice or mashed potatoes.

Prep time: 15 minutes
Cook time: 1 hour and 15 minutes

BASTE: To moisten foods during cooking with pan drippings or special sauce to add flavor and prevent dryness.

Beef Burgundy Stew

This is very easy, but takes a while to cook.

> 2 pounds of lean stewing meat, cut into bite size pieces
> 1 cup burgundy wine
> 1 can (2.8 oz.) French fried onions
> 1 can (10-3/4 oz.) condensed cream of mushroom soup
> 1 can (10-3/4 oz.) condensed cream of celery soup
> 8 oz. sliced button mushrooms (approx. 2 cups)

Preheat the oven to 325° F. In a large skillet over high heat, quickly brown the meat. (You aren't trying to really cook it through at this point, just browning to provide flavor.) Combine all ingredients in a deep baking dish sprayed with cooking spray. Cook, uncovered, for 3 hours, stirring every hour.

Serves: 4 - 6

 This stew is great served over egg noodles.

 Prep time: 10 minutes
Cook time: 3 hours

Traditional Beef Lasagna

Mamma Mia! Here's a taste of little Italy.

1 lb. lean ground beef
1 can (6 oz.) plain tomato paste
1 can (28 oz.) crushed tomatoes in puree
1 Tablespoon garlic, chopped
3 Tablespoons granulated sugar
1 Tablespoon dried oregano
1 Tablespoon old hickory smoked salt (optional)
3 Tablespoons dried parsley
1 Tablespoon dried chives
1 tub (15 oz.) Ricotta cheese (you'll have extra)
8 oz. Mozzarella cheese, grated
1 package lasagna noodles (you'll only need 9)

In a large skillet over medium-high heat, brown the ground beef, drain, and set aside. In a large saucepan, mix together the next 8 ingredients and simmer for 25 minutes. Add the beef and mix well. Meanwhile, boil the lasagna noodles until they are "al dente", or still a little firm. Drain the noodles and lay them flat on aluminum foil so they won't stick together. Spray a 9"x13" pan with cooking spray and preheat the oven to 425° F. Spread a little bit of the sauce in the bottom of the pan, then top with 3 noodles set lengthwise in the pan, side by side. Spread some of the Ricotta cheese on the noodles with your fingertips, then top with some of the sauce. Sprinkle some Mozzarella over the sauce and continue building the lasagna by repeating the noodles, Ricotta, sauce, Mozzarella layers. *(This recipe can be made several hours or a day ahead, even frozen, up to this point.)* Bake, covered, for 20 minutes, then uncovered for 10 more minutes. If frozen, bake for 1 hour, uncovered during the last 10 minutes.

Prep time: 30 minutes
Cook time: 30 minutes

MOZZARELLA CHEESE (Italy): Pale ivory in color with a mild and delicate flavor. Somewhat soft and creamy, melts easily. The pizza cheese, it is used frequently in Italian foods and sandwiches.

Crusted Lamb Chops

This versatile bread crumb coating works well on just about any cut of lamb.

2/3 cup plain bread crumbs
1/2 cup fresh parsley, finely chopped
3 cloves of garlic, minced
2 shallots, finely chopped
4 Tablespoons (1/2 stick) unsalted butter, melted
2 teaspoons dry mustard
1/8 teaspoon cayenne pepper
8 lamb chops, 1" thick
   (or, 4 lamb shoulder chops or leg of lamb steaks)

Preheat oven to 500° F and line a roasting pan with foil. In a shallow dish, mix together the bread crumbs, parsley, garlic, and shallots. In a separate dish, combine the melted butter, mustard, and cayenne pepper. Season the lamb with salt and pepper to taste. Dip both sides of each chop into the butter mixture, then both sides into the bread crumb mixture, gently pressing to be sure coating sticks. Place in a roasting pan and bake, uncovered, until lamb is at your desired doneness (about 16 to 20 minutes).

Serves: 4

Prep time: 20 minutes
Cook time: 16 - 20 minutes

PARSLEY: Best when used fresh, but can also be used dried. This herb is used as a garnish or to season fish, omelets, soups, meats, stuffing and mixed greens.

Shepherd's Pie

If ground lamb is not available, substitute ground beef.

3/4 to 1 lb. ground lamb
1 cup yellow onion, chopped
2 large garlic cloves, minced
1 can (14-1/2 oz.) Italian-style stewed tomatoes
1/2 teaspoon dried rosemary, crushed or crumbled
2 cups mashed potatoes, room temperature
3 Tablespoons Parmesan cheese, grated

Preheat oven to 500° F. Over medium heat in a heavy medium size saucepan, stir lamb, onion, and garlic until lamb is light brown and onion is tender, about 5 minutes. Increase heat to high and mix in stewed tomatoes with their juices and cook until most of the liquid evaporates, breaking up tomatoes with the back of the spoon, about 10 minutes. Season with salt & pepper to taste. Spoon mixture into 9 inch round glass pie plate. Spread mashed potatoes atop the lamb mixture, covering completely. Sprinkle with cheese. Bake until potatoes are light golden, about 15 minutes.

Serves: 4

Prep time: 20 minutes
Cook time: 15 minutes

ROSEMARY: Very aromatic herb, used fresh or dried. Frequently used to season lamb, beef, poultry, stuffing, eggs, and bread.

Baked Pork Chops

Yes, Martha . . . a can of condensed soup! Shortcuts are essential.
Suggested side dishes: mashed potatoes a must,
and green beans a plus!

4 thick pork chops, boneless
1 egg
1/2 cup plain bread crumbs
1/2 teaspoon garlic salt
1 teaspoon parsley
1/2 teaspoon oregano
1 can (10-3/4 oz.) condensed cream of mushroom soup

Preheat oven to 350° F. In a small bowl, beat the egg. Dip pork chops in egg and coat both sides with bread crumbs. Place the chops in a baking dish coated with cooking spray. Sprinkle garlic salt, parsley, and oregano on top of the chops. Cover with foil and bake for 45 minutes. Remove from oven and cover them with cream of mushroom soup. Replace foil and bake for another 20 minutes.

Serves: 4

 Prep time: 10 minutes
Cook time: 1 hour and 5 minutes

BBQ Pork Ribs

Fair warning: For the tastiest and most tender results, plan to start these the morning of (or even the day before) you will serve them.

Ribs:
          2 racks of pork ribs
          Your favorite BBQ sauce (or try the one below)

Place the ribs in a large stockpot and cover with water. Bring to a boil, then turn the heat down a bit so the water is just barely boiling. Cook this way for 1 hour. Drain and slather in BBQ sauce, then refrigerate all day or over night. Just before you're ready to serve, grill the ribs for 10 minutes (or just until heated through).

Sauce:
          1/2 cup ketchup
          1/2 cup water
          1/4 cup cider vinegar
          3 Tablespoons granulated sugar
          1 teaspoon chili powder
          1 teaspoon salt
          1/8 teaspoon black pepper

Mix together all ingredients. Store in refrigerator until ready to use.

Yields: 1 cup sauce, ribs recipe serves 4 (can easily be doubled)

 CHILL and marinate overnight

 Prep time: 5 minutes
Cook time: Ribs - 1 hour and 10 minutes

 MERLOT also goes well with:
Cheese: aged cheeses
Meat: venison, barbeque
Seafood: grilled swordfish
Veggies: black beans

BLT Tortillas

I loved BLT sandwiches as a kid.
Now that I am more sophisticated (right!) I moved on to tortillas.

8 slices of bacon
8 flour tortillas (small)
1/2 cup Cheddar cheese, shredded
1/2 cup salsa
1/2 cup sour cream
1/2 cup lettuce

In large skillet place bacon flat. Heat over medium high. Turn bacon over every 2 minutes a total of 4 times. For the next 4 minutes tilt skillet so all bacon is submersed in grease. For crispier bacon cook a few minutes longer. Place tortillas flat on individual plates. Add 1 Tablespoon of Cheddar cheese, 2 slices cooked bacon, 1 Tablespoon of salsa and 1 Tablespoon of sour cream. Heat in microwave for 15 seconds until flour tortilla is warm and cheese is slightly melted. Top with lettuce. Fold in half and enjoy.

Serves: 4

 Sprinkle some salt in the skillet before adding bacon and there will be less grease splattered. Effective with any meat.

 Prep time: 10 minutes
Cook time: 14 minutes

 Never cook bacon in the nude.

Ham & Broccoli Casserole

This can be assembled ahead of time (even frozen) then baked just before serving.

3 large heads of fresh broccoli, or, use 2 bags (14 oz. each) frozen florets
2 lbs. pre-cooked hickory or maple ham, or, turkey cured to taste like ham, chopped
1/4 cup dried, minced onions
1 can (10-3/4 oz.) condensed cream of mushroom soup
8 oz. light sour cream
2/3 box bacon flavored crackers, crushed

Cut the fresh broccoli into florets. Whether fresh or frozen, steam the florets for just 7 minutes (should remain bright green and firm). Spray the bottom of a 9" x 13" baking dish with cooking spray and spread the florets evenly across the bottom. Preheat the oven to 350° F. Spread the bite sized chunks of ham over the broccoli. In a small bowl, mix together the onion, soup, and sour cream and blend well, then pour over the ham and broccoli. Top with the crushed crackers and bake, uncovered, for 30 minutes.

Serves: 6

 Best served over steamed white rice.

 Prep time: 15 minutes
Cook time: 30 minutes

Pork and Kraut

An easy stew that is awesome! A traditional New Year's Meal . . .
at least, it is for Lithuanians.

2 pounds pork tenderloin, cut in half lengthwise
3 cups yellow onion, sliced
4 cups potatoes, peeled and cubed (1-2" pieces)
2 cups baby-cut carrots
1 can (15 oz.) sauerkraut (Bavarian Style, sweet)
1/2 Tablespoon garlic salt
1/2 Tablespoon fresh ground pepper
4 cups water

Preheat oven to 350° F. Place pork loins in a large covered pot. Add onions, potatoes, carrots, sauerkraut, garlic salt, pepper, and cover all with water. Cook 2 hours and 15 minutes. Remove from oven. Using a fork, pull chunks off the pork and allow to baste while cooling.

Serves: 4

Prep time: 10 minutes
Cook time: 2 hours and 15 minutes

ZINFANDEL also goes well with:
Cheese: aged cheeses
Meat: pork, sausage, stew
Seafood: blackened fish
Veggies: tomatoes, eggplant

Vegetarian Bean Burgers

Worried about digestion? Have no fear . . . just add 2 stalks of chopped celery to this recipe.

2 cans (16 oz. each) butter beans, drained and rinsed
1/2 cup red onion, diced
1 cup tomatoes, chopped
2 Tablespoons all purpose flour
1 Tablespoon garlic, minced
1/2 Tablespoon cumin
1 egg, beaten
1/2 cup Cheddar cheese, shredded
1/4 teaspoon salt
1/4 cup vegetable oil

In medium bowl, mash both beans together. Mix in red onion, tomatoes, flour, garlic, cumin, egg, cheese, and salt. Divide into 6 equal parts and shape into patties. Heat oil in a large skillet over medium-high heat. Fry patties until golden brown, about 4 minutes on each side. Drain on paper towel.

Serves: 6

 Prep time: 25 minutes
Cook time: 16 minutes

Alfredo Lasagna with Vegetables

You can substitute the 2 cups of red bell pepper with any fleshy vegetable. For example, 1 cup of fresh sliced mushrooms and 1 cup of fresh sliced zucchini. You choose!

1/4 cup olive oil light
2 cups red bell pepper, diced
2 cups yellow onion, diced
1 Tablespoon parsley, dried
1 teaspoon oregano, dried
1 teaspoon basil, dried
2 cups half and half
3 cups Ricotta cheese
1 cup Parmesan cheese, grated
1/2 teaspoon salt
1 package lasagna noodles (you'll only need 9, cooked)
2 cups Mozzarella cheese, shredded

Preheat oven to 350° F. In a large sauté pan, heat oil over medium heat. Add red bell pepper and onion. Sauté for 8 - 10 minutes until tender. Turn off heat. In same pan, add parsley, oregano, basil, half and half, Ricotta cheese, Parmesan cheese, and salt. Mix thoroughly. Coat 9" x 13" pan with cooking spray. Layer the bottom of pan with 3 noodles side by side. Spread 1/3 of mixture evenly on noodles. Place 3 more noodles on mixture and spread another 1/3 of mixture. Repeat one more time. Now sprinkle Mozzarella cheese evenly on top. Bake for 40 minutes or until cheese is golden.

Serves: 9

Prep time: 40 minutes
Cook time: 50 minutes

RICOTTA CHEESE (Italy): A white, rindless cheese with mild, semi-sweet nutty flavor and creamy texture. Keeps 2 weeks. Used in many Italian dishes.

Kris' Artichoke and Caper Pasta Sauce

*This has been one of our family's favorite pasta dishes for years –
try it and you'll see why.*

1/4 cup extra virgin olive oil
1 medium size yellow onion, diced
1 can (14 oz.) quartered artichoke hearts, drained and
  sliced
2 Tablespoons capers, chopped in half
2 cans (14.5 oz. each) diced tomatoes with Italian
  herbs, drained
16 oz. penne pasta
1/4 cup grated Parmesan cheese
2 Tablespoons fresh parsley, finely chopped

In a large skillet, heat the olive oil and sauté the onion until tender.
Add the artichoke hearts and cook, over medium heat, until slightly
golden. Stir in the capers and tomatoes. Season to taste with salt and
pepper. Continue cooking for 20 minutes, stirring frequently.
Meanwhile, boil the pasta according to the package directions. Serve
the pasta, covered with the sauce, and top with Parmesan cheese and
fresh parsley.

Serves: 4 - 6

Prep time: 20 minutes
Cook time: 15 minutes

CAPERS: Small, pickled flower buds of a Mediterranean shrub
used as a pungent condiment in sauces, relishes, with fish and
other dishes.

Broccoli Cannelloni

Martha would nail me on my cooking etiquette . . .
I use my fingers to stuff the tubes!

1 Tablespoon oil
12 - 14 uncooked cannelloni/manicotti tubes
4 cups of broccoli florets, minced
1/2 cup milk
1 Tablespoon garlic, minced
1 tub (15 oz.) Ricotta cheese
1/4 cup Parmesan cheese, grated
1 can (15 oz.) tomato sauce
1 can (14.5 oz.) diced tomatoes, Italian style
1 cup Mozzarella cheese, shredded

Preheat oven to 350° F. Bring a pot of water to boil, adding the oil to the water so the pasta tubes do not stick together. Boil the cannelloni tubes until al dente. Drain and rinse in warm water. Meanwhile, cook broccoli florets until tender (in microwave or in small saucepan) and drain. In a medium bowl, mix milk, garlic, Ricotta cheese, Parmesan cheese, and cooked broccoli. Open pasta tubes and pipe in the filling. Some people use kitchen instruments . . . I use my fingers. Place filled tubes in a 9" x 13" casserole dish, creating two rows. Pour tomato sauce and diced tomatoes across the tops of the cannelloni. Sprinkle Mozzarella cheese on top of sauce. Bake for 30 minutes or until cheese is golden.

Serves: 6

Prep time: 30 minutes
Cook time: 30 minutes

Cheese-Stuffed Manicotti

This is a great "do-ahead" dish and perfect for entertaining. Filling the manicotti tubes can get a bit messy, but it's really easy once you get the hang of it.

12 - 14 uncooked manicotti/cannelloni tubes
1/2 cup onion, finely chopped
3 garlic cloves, minced
1 cup Mozzarella cheese, shredded and divided
1/2 cup Parmesan cheese, grated and divided
1/2 teaspoon black pepper
1-1/2 teaspoons dried Italian seasoning
1 tub (15 oz.) Ricotta cheese
6 oz. garden veggie cream cheese, softened
4 oz. plain cream cheese, softened
1/2 package (about 5 oz.) frozen chopped spinach,
    thawed, drained & squeezed dry
1 jar (28 oz.) of pasta or marinara sauce

Preheat oven to 350° F. Spray a 9"x13" pan with cooking spray. Boil manicotti shells according to package directions and drain. Coat a non-stick skillet with cooking spray and sauté onion and garlic over medium-high heat for 3 minutes. Remove from heat and set aside. In a large bowl or food processor, combine 1/2 cup of Mozzarella, 1/4 cup of Parmesan, Italian seasoning, pepper, Ricotta, and softened cream cheeses. Beat at medium mixer speed until smooth. Stir in onion/garlic and spinach, mixing until well blended. Gently spoon into manicotti shells (don't worry if one or two split during filling). Pour half of the jar of pasta sauce into the pan and arrange filled shells atop the sauce. Top with the rest of the sauce. *NOTE: Recipe can be made up to this point and refrigerated several hours before baking.* Cover with foil and bake 25 minutes. Remove foil and sprinkle with remaining cheeses. Bake, uncovered, another 5 minutes.

Serves: 6

Prep time: 35 minutes
Cook time: 30 minutes

Spaghetti Sauce & Turkey Balls

Tasty, healthy and fun to say. Serve with some different noodles like Ziti. Ground beef can be substituted for the Turkey.

Sauce:
      1 can (6 oz.) tomato paste
      1 can (14.5 oz.) crushed tomatoes
      1 can (15 oz.) tomato sauce
      1/2 teaspoon oregano
      1/2 teaspoon basil
      1 teaspoon parsley
      1 Tablespoon garlic, minced
      15 oz. water (use empty tomato sauce can)
      8 oz. fresh mushrooms, sliced (optional)

In a large saucepan, mix all ingredients above. Simmer over low heat.

Turkey Balls:
      1-1/3 lbs. of lean ground turkey
      1 egg
      1/3 cup Parmesan cheese, grated
      1/2 Tablespoon garlic, minced
      1/2 Tablespoon parsley
      1 teaspoon basil
      1 teaspoon oregano

Combine meat, egg, cheese, and herbs. Mix well. Roll into 2 inch balls, yielding 12 meat balls. Place in sauce. Let solidify for 10 minutes before stirring. Cook for an hour. Stir occasionally.

Serves: 8

Prep time: 20 minutes
Cook time: 1 hour

Christine's Asian Style Marinade

Fair Warning: Plan to make this marinade the day before serving to let the flavors really soak into the meat. The recipe below features chicken, but this works well with just about any meat.

6 boneless, skinless chicken breasts
2 Tablespoons sesame seeds
1/2 cup soy sauce
1 can (8 oz.) plain tomato sauce
1/2 cup vegetable oil (or canola or safflower)
1/4 cup granulated sugar
3 green onions, chopped
1 teaspoon garlic, minced

Clean and remove any fat from the chicken and set aside. In a dry skillet over medium heat, stir the sesame seeds until they become golden and very aromatic. Remove from heat and cool. In a large bowl, combine all the remaining ingredients and the sesame seeds and stir well. Immerse the chicken in the marinade and chill in the fridge overnight.
Preheat the oven to 350° F and spray the bottom of a 9"x13" baking dish with cooking spray. Put the chicken in the pan and spoon a bit of the marinade over each breast. Bake, uncovered, for 45 minutes.

Serves: 6

 CHILL and marinate overnight

 Prep time: 20 minutes
Cook time: 45 minutes

 MARINADE: To allow food to stand in a liquid to tenderize or add flavor.

Beer Marinated Smoked Chicken

Fair warning: For the best flavor, start this the day before or at least the morning you'll be serving.

1 bottle of beer (any kind)
3/4 cup vegetable oil (or canola or corn)
1 large yellow onion, peeled and sliced
2 shallots, peeled and chopped
2 cloves garlic, peeled and minced
1 bunch fresh cilantro, stemmed and chopped
2 teaspoons salt
1-1/2 teaspoons crushed black pepper
1/8 teaspoon cayenne pepper
6 boneless, skinless chicken breasts

Combine all ingredients in a large bowl and marinate for at least 2 hours or up to 1 day.

Note: Smoking the chicken really adds to the flavor, but is an optional step, so just skip it if you don't have a smoker.

If you choose to smoke the chicken, do so on a barbecue grill for approximately 7 minutes on each side, then return the chicken to the marinade for 1 more hour, minimum. Barbecue the chicken about 4 minutes per side – be sure not to overcook!

The chicken can be placed in the marinade up to a day ahead and then grilled just before serving. Serve the chicken breasts whole, or slice them up for excellent fajitas.

Serves: 6

 Marinating is a cinch if you use a plastic zipper bag. The meat stays in the marinade and it's easy to turn and rearrange. Clean up is easy too – just toss the bag!

 CHILL and marinate overnight

 Prep time: 20 minutes
Cook time: 8 - 10 minutes

Thom's Chicken Enchiladas

These can be made ahead of time and then baked just before guests arrive.

4 boneless, skinless chicken breasts
(or one whole roasted chicken)
1 small onion, diced
1/4 cup extra virgin olive oil
3 roma tomatoes, diced
Pinch of dried basil and oregano
2 dozen corn tortillas
2 cups Monterey Jack cheese, shredded
1 can (10-3/4 oz.) condensed cream of mushroom soup
1/2 cup milk
1/2 cup sour cream
1 small can chopped green chilies (optional)

Preheat the oven to 350° F. Clean the chicken and remove any fat, then bake the breasts for 40 minutes. Let cool slightly. Shred or chop the chicken into bite size pieces. In a skillet, sauté the onion in olive oil. Add tomatoes and sauté until soft. Add chicken, basil, and oregano and stir until just heated through. Spray the bottom of a 9"x13" baking dish with cooking spray. In a tortilla, place some cheese and meat mixture, then roll up the tortilla and place in the baking dish. Repeat until all chicken is used and pan is full. In a small bowl, mix together the mushroom soup, sour cream, milk, and green chilies. Pour over enchiladas and top with remaining cheese. Bake, covered, for 30 minutes, then uncovered for 10 more minutes.

Serves: 6

 Warm the tortillas first – they'll be more pliable and less likely to split or break.

 Prep time: 35 minutes
Cook time: 1 hour and 20 minutes

Chicken with Mushrooms and Balsamic Vinegar

This dish comes together very quickly, so it's a good choice if you're pressed for time.

1/2 cup all purpose flour
1/4 teaspoon salt
1/4 teaspoon pepper
4 boneless, skinless chicken breasts
2 Tablespoons extra virgin olive oil
4 garlic cloves, peeled and minced
8 oz. mushrooms, sliced
3/4 cups chicken broth
1/4 cup Balsamic vinegar
2 bay leaves
1/4 teaspoon dried thyme
1 Tablespoon unsalted butter

Place the flour in a shallow dish and season with salt and pepper. Next, dredge the chicken in the flour mixture. In a large skillet, heat the oil over medium heat. Add the chicken and cook until browned on one side, approximately 4 to 5 minutes. Turn the chicken over, then add the garlic and mushrooms. Continue cooking 4 to 5 more minutes, moving the garlic and mushrooms around in the skillet. Add the chicken broth, vinegar, bay leaves, and thyme. Cover tightly, reduce the heat to medium-low and cook for 10 minutes, turning the chicken occasionally. Transfer the chicken to a serving platter and cover with foil to keep warm. Raise the heat to medium and cook the pan juices, uncovered, for 7 more minutes. Remove and discard the bay leaves, add salt and pepper to taste, then stir in the butter until melted. Spoon the sauce over the chicken and serve.

Serves: 4

 Cook time: 30 - 35 minutes

 BAY LEAVES: Turkish leaves release a pungent flavor good in vegetable dishes, fish and seafood, stews, and pickles.

Chicken Tenders

Great for the kids. Delicious as an appetizer, or on our Cobb Salad. Serve with our Honey Mustard Dressing recipe.

3 boneless, skinless chicken breasts
1/2 cup bread crumbs
1/4 cup Parmesan cheese, grated
1 teaspoon garlic salt
1 Tablespoon dried parsley
1/2 teaspoon dried basil
2 eggs

Preheat oven to 400° F. Cut chicken breast into 1-1/2 inch size pieces. In medium bowl, mix bread crumbs, Parmesan cheese, garlic salt, parsley, and basil. In another bowl, beat eggs. Dip chicken into egg first and then coat entirely in bread crumb mixture. Place coated chicken pieces in a lightly greased 9" x13" casserole dish in single layer. Cover with foil and bake for 10 minutes. Remove foil and bake another 10 minutes uncovered.

Serves: 6

 Prep time: 10 minutes
Cook time: 20 minutes

Karen's Coq Au Vin

Chicken in wine sauce . . . a dinner party favorite . . . puts everyone in a good mood!

2 Tablespoons olive oil light
5 ounces pearl onions
4 chicken breasts, boneless and skinless
1 Tablespoon garlic, minced
8 oz. fresh mushrooms, sliced
1-1/2 cups red wine (I recommend Pinot Noir)
1 cup chicken broth
1 Tablespoon cornstarch

In a large deep sauté pot, heat the oil over medium low heat. Add onions, cover, and cook for 10 to 15 minutes until tender. Remove and set aside. Turn the heat up to medium and brown chicken for 5 minutes on each side. When browned, set chicken aside. Add garlic and mushrooms to the pot and sauté for 3 minutes. Add chicken and onions back into the pot. Add the wine and chicken broth. Cook, covered, for 20 minutes over medium heat. Lift chicken and vegetables to serving dish. Bring remaining liquids to a boil. Add cornstarch and stir over heat for approximately 4 minutes until thick. Pour thickened broth over chicken and vegetables, and serve.

Serves: 4

Prep time: 10 minutes
Cook time: 50 minutes

PINOT NOIR also goes well with:
Cheese: goat cheese, Brie
Meat: duck, lamb
Seafood: salmon, tuna
Veggie: mushrooms

Margo's Cranberry Chicken

Martha, go ahead and take a whack at this recipe. You'll need a mallet or a hammer.

4 boneless, skinless chicken breasts
1/2 cup (1 stick) unsalted butter, melted
1 can (16 oz.) whole berry cranberry sauce
2 cups Italian (or plain) bread crumbs
Toothpicks

Clean and remove any fat from the chicken. Place each breast between 2 sheets of plastic wrap and pound until flat with a mallet or hammer. Preheat the oven to 350° F. Set the butter, bread crumbs and cranberry sauce in separate bowls and spray a deep baking dish with cooking spray. One by one, dredge the breasts in the melted butter, then coat well with the bread crumbs, pressing gently to adhere. Spoon a generous amount of the cranberry sauce across the middle width of the breast, then carefully roll it up and secure it with one or two toothpicks. Set the breasts in the baking dish and drizzle with remaining melted butter. Bake, uncovered, for 45 minutes.
For more servings, simply increase the number of chicken breasts; do not double the rest of the ingredients unless you are preparing this for 8 or more.

Serves: 4

 Be sure to caution your guests about the toothpicks in the chicken.

 Prep time: 20 minutes
Cook time: 45 minutes

Creamy Chicken Stew

This is an easy, casual dinner favorite. I like to open a bottle of Sauvignon Blanc and start this meal with a green salad and have some French bread on the side. This stew is real comfort food and is great served over egg noodles.

2 medium size russet potatoes
2 large carrots
2 medium to large size leeks
3 Tablespoons unsalted butter
2 Tablespoons fresh parsley, finely chopped
2 teaspoons fresh rosemary, finely chopped
2 cloves of garlic, chopped
1-3/4 cups chicken broth
1 can (10-3/4 oz.) condensed cream of chicken soup
1/2 cup heavy cream
2 cups cooked chicken, diced

Peel the potatoes and carrots and slice them into bite size pieces. Wash the leeks well and cut off the dark green ends. Slice them lengthwise, then slice crosswise into approximately 1/2 inch wide strips. Melt the butter in a large stockpot over medium heat and add the chopped vegetables plus the herbs and garlic. Sauté for 10 minutes to soften the vegetables. Add the chicken broth and bring to a boil. Cover the pot and reduce heat to low. Simmer until vegetables are tender, about 20 minutes. Mix in the soup and cream, then add the chicken and stir well. Simmer for 5 more minutes, then season to taste with salt & pepper.

Serves: 6

Prep time: 20 minutes
Cook time: 40 minutes

Hot Chicken Salad Casserole

Just like cold chicken salad, but serve this dish heated through!

4 boneless, skinless chicken breasts
1 can (10-3/4 oz.) cream of chicken soup
1/2 cup mayonnaise
1 Tablespoon lemon juice
2 cups celery, chopped
1 cup onion, chopped
4 hard boiled eggs, chopped
1/2 teaspoon salt
1 cup Cheddar cheese, grated

Preheat oven to 375° F. Boil the chicken breasts in a large pot of water for 25 minutes. Cool chicken meat and cut into 1 inch cubes. In a 9" x 13" casserole dish, combine chicken cubes, soup, mayonnaise, lemon juice, celery, onions, boiled eggs, and salt. Mix thoroughly. Sprinkle Cheddar cheese across top evenly. Bake for 20-25 minutes until cheese is golden.

Serves: 6

Prep time: 30 minutes
Cook time: 50 minutes

Marsala Parmesan Chicken

This recipe would still be great if you chose to omit the wine.

1/8 teaspoon dried thyme
1/4 teaspoon paprika
1/4 teaspoon garlic salt
1 Tablespoon dried parsley
1/4 cup Parmesan cheese, grated
1/3 cup Italian (or plain) bread crumbs
1/3 cup water
4 boneless, skinless chicken breasts
2 Tablespoons extra virgin olive oil
1/4 cup (1/2 stick) unsalted butter, melted
1/3 cup Marsala wine

Preheat the oven to 350° F. In a large plastic zipper bag, combine the first 6 ingredients. Spray a glass baking dish with cooking spray and pour in the water. Clean and remove any fat from the chicken, then shake 1 piece at a time in the plastic bag, coating well with the bread crumb mixture. Arrange the chicken pieces in the baking dish and top with a little bit of the leftover bread crumb mixture, then salt and pepper to taste. Drizzle the oil and butter over the chicken and bake, uncovered, for 30 minutes. Lower the oven temperature to 325° F and pour the wine over the chicken. Bake for another 15 minutes covered with a lid or foil.

For more servings, simply increase the number of chicken breasts. Do not double the rest of the ingredients unless you are preparing this for 8 or more.

Serves: 4

Prep time: 20 minutes
Cook time: 45 minutes

Turkey Tetrazzini

This is a great way to use up leftover turkey after Thanksgiving!

8 oz. uncooked linguini noodles
1/2 cup slivered almonds
1 Tablespoon unsalted butter
8 oz. sliced mushrooms
1/3 cup shallots, chopped
2 cups chicken broth
1/4 cup sherry
1/3 cup all purpose flour
2 cups low-fat or fat-free milk (cold)
1/8 teaspoon ground nutmeg
2 cups cooked turkey breast (or chicken), chopped
1/2 cup + 2 Tablespoons Parmesan cheese, grated

Preheat oven to 350° F and spray a deep baking dish with cooking spray. Prepare the pasta according to the package instructions, cooking until just soft. Drain and place in the bottom of the baking dish. Toast the almonds on a baking sheet in the oven for 5 minutes, or until just slightly golden, then sprinkle atop the noodles. In a large skillet, melt butter, and sauté mushrooms and shallots until tender. Reduce heat to simmer and add broth and sherry. In a medium bowl, whisk together the flour and milk until smooth. Slowly add this to the mushroom mixture, whisking to keep it smooth. Simmer for 5 more minutes, then add the nutmeg plus salt and pepper to taste. Stir in the turkey and 1/2 cup Parmesan cheese. Simmer for 1 minute. Pour the mushroom mixture over the noodles and almonds. Top with the remaining 2 Tablespoons of Parmesan cheese. (*Can be done several hours or up to 1 day ahead to this point*) Bake, uncovered, 35 minutes. Let stand 10 minutes.

Serves: 6 - 8

 When draining, run cooked linguini noodles under HOT water to help prevent stickiness.

 Prep time: 20 minutes
Cook time: 35 minutes

Halibut with Roasted Tomatoes

If they are available, try using yellow or orange colored tomatoes in addition to regular red ones for a nice splash of color.

1/4 cup extra virgin olive oil
1 Tablespoon + 1 teaspoon balsamic vinegar
1 Tablespoon fresh basil, finely chopped
1 green onion, finely chopped (white & light green parts only)
2 teaspoons fresh cilantro, finely chopped
1/8 teaspoon (approx.) saffron threads (optional)*
4 cups tomatoes, cut into chunks
4 halibut fillets (8 oz. each, about 1 inch thick)

Preheat oven to 450° F and spray a large baking dish with cooking spray. In a small bowl, combine the oil, vinegar, basil, onion, cilantro & saffron and whisk to blend. Let stand for 10 minutes. Meanwhile, place the tomato chunks on the bottom of the dish and lightly sprinkle with salt and pepper. Next, set the halibut fillets atop the tomatoes and lightly sprinkle them with salt and pepper. Whisk dressing once more and pour over the fish. Bake, uncovered, for 10 minutes or until fish is opaque in the center. Serve the tomatoes over the fish and spoon the pan juices atop.
This recipe can easily be doubled.

Serves: 4

*Saffron gives this dish a lovely golden hue, but since it can be a bit pricey, don't worry if you elect to leave it out.

Prep time: 20 minutes
Cook time: 10 minutes

SAFFRON: Thin orange-yellow threads, this spice is commonly used to flavor or color foods such as soup, fish, chicken, rice and fancy breads.

Grilled Pesto Salmon

If salmon is not available or too highly priced, consider substituting steelhead trout.

3/4 lb. salmon fillet (with skin on)
1/3 cup prepared pesto sauce
(see Premo Pesto Sauce recipe or use purchased)
1/4 cup Italian style bread crumbs

Turn on grill, warm to medium heat. Place salmon on a large sheet of aluminum foil, skin side down. Spread the pesto sauce on the top of the salmon, then sprinkle the bread crumbs atop. Wrap the salmon in the foil and grill for 8 minutes per side.
This recipe can easily be doubled.

Serves: 2

Prep time: 5 minutes
Cook time: 16 minutes

CHARDONNAY also goes well with:
Cheese: Asiago
Meat: chicken, pork loin
Seafood: salmon, crab
Veggie: potato, avocado

Soy-Ginger Salmon

Salmon is one of the best fish for you and this is an easy way to prepare it.

2 Tablespoons vegetable oil, divided
2 salmon fillets (6 oz. each), skin removed
1/4 cup yellow onion, finely chopped
2 Tablespoons firmly packed brown sugar
3 Tablespoons soy sauce
2 Tablespoons white wine
2 Tablespoons lemon juice
1 teaspoon garlic, minced
1 teaspoon freshly grated ginger root

Heat 1 Tablespoon of oil over high heat in a large skillet. Add the salmon, cover, and reduce heat to medium-high and cook for 6 minutes, turning over half way. Transfer the salmon to a plate and cover with foil to keep warm. In the same skillet, add the remaining oil and sauté the onion for 1 minute over medium heat. In a small bowl, whisk together all remaining ingredients then add to the skillet. Bring sauce to a boil and return salmon to the pan and cook for 2 minutes, turning once.

Serves: 2

Prep time: 12 minutes
Cook time: 9 minutes

GINGER: A pungent root, this aromatic spice is sold fresh, dried, ground, pickled, and crystallized. Used in preserves, cakes, cookies, soups, meat, and fish dishes.

Scallops on a Skewer

Try these scallops . . . this recipe is so easy! Side dish suggestion: serve with our Parmesan Potato Wedges recipe.

2 Tablespoons maple syrup
1 Tablespoon soy sauce
1 Tablespoon Dijon mustard
20 large sea scallops
5 bacon slices

In medium bowl, combine maple syrup, soy sauce, and mustard. Add scallops and stir gently to coat. Marinate in refrigerator for 1 hour. *Note: If yours are wooden skewers, soak them in water for 30 minutes before using them to broil food. Don't discard marinade -- use it to baste while broiling.*
Cut bacon slices into 4 pieces. Wrap bacon piece around marinated scallop. Thread scallop onto skewers leaving space in between for bacon to cook. Coat broiler pan with cooking spray and place scallops on top. Broil 4 minutes and baste with reserved marinade. Broil another 4 minutes or until bacon is done.

Serves: 4

 CHILL and marinate for 1 hour

 Prep time: 20 minutes
Cook time: 8 minutes

Shrimp Scampi

I use Chardonnay as my wine choice. Since I only need 1/4 cup for this recipe, I then have plenty to drink with the dish. You can use either fresh or dried herbs.

1 Tablespoon of olive oil light
1 Tablespoon butter
2 Tablespoons garlic, minced
1/4 cup dry white wine
1 teaspoon dried parsley
1/4 teaspoon dried oregano
1/4 teaspoon dried basil
1 pound shrimp, peeled and deveined
1 Tablespoon lemon juice
1/4 teaspoon salt

In a large sauté pan, heat oil and butter over low heat. Add and sauté the garlic until golden. Add wine, parsley, oregano, and basil. Cook until wine is reduced significantly. Add shrimp, lemon juice, and salt. Toss until shrimp are pink, several minutes.

Serves: 4

Substitution of fresh herbs:
2 Tablespoons minced parsley
1/2 Tablespoon chopped basil
1/2 Tablespoon chopped oregano

Prep time: 15 minutes
Cook time: 15 minutes

Tuna Steaks

No more casseroles. Tuna does taste great! Serve with Thai peanut sauce, ginger flavored dressing, or wasabi to give it a kick.

1/2 cup white sesame seeds
1 Tablespoon coarsely cracked black pepper
1/4 teaspoon salt
4 yellowfin tuna steaks (5 oz. each)
2 Tablespoons cooking oil
1/4 cup cooking oil

In a small dish, combine sesame seed, cracked pepper, and salt. Rub entire tuna with 2 Tablespoons of oil. Press seasoning mixture onto both sides of the tuna steaks. In a large sauté pan, heat 1/4 cup cooking oil over medium high heat. Sear tuna for 3 minutes on each side until medium rare. Serve with one of the suggestions listed above.

Serves: 4

 Prep time: 10 minutes
Cook time: 6 minutes

Desserts

Berry Good Pie

Martha . . . I cheated again. Pie crust is too hard to make when I can simply buy it at the grocery store ready to bake.

2/3 cup granulated sugar
2 Tablespoons cornstarch
2/3 cup water
1 Tablespoon lemon juice
1 cup (1/2 pint) sliced strawberries
2 cups (1 pint) blueberries
1 cup (1/2 pint) blackberries
2 ready-to-bake crusts for 9" pie

Preheat oven to 425° F. In a medium pan over medium heat, stir in sugar, cornstarch, and water. Bring to a boil. Add lemon juice and half of the berries. Cook and stir for another 3 minutes until thick. Remove from heat and stir in remaining berries. Cool for 10 minutes. Pour into the lower crust of a 9 inch pie plate. (Please follow directions on ready-to-bake pie crust package). Top the pie with second crust and crimp edges (see tip below). Cut 6 slits in top of crust. Bake for 35 to 40 minutes until lightly brown on top.

Serves: 8

 Keep the juices in the pie by folding the top crust over the lower crust before crimping.

 Prep time: 15 minutes
Cook time: 35 - 40 minutes

 CRIMP: To seal the edges of a two-crust pie either by pinching them at intervals with the fingers or by pressing them together with the tines of a fork.

Caramel Apple Pie

This is perhaps the best apple pie recipe I've ever come across.

1 refrigerated 9"pie crust
2 to 2-1/2 lbs. Golden Delicious apples (about 6)
1/4 cup all purpose flour
1-1/4 cups granulated sugar
1/4 cup + 2 Tablespoons water
3 Tablespoons unsalted butter
1 Tablespoon ground cinnamon
3/4 cup all purpose flour
6 Tablespoons granulated sugar
1 teaspoon pumpkin pie spice
1/4 teaspoon salt
6 Tablespoons (3/4 stick) unsalted butter

Preheat the oven to 375° F. Roll out the pie crust and transfer to a deep dish pie plate. Peel, core, and slice the apples into 3/4 inch wedges. In a large bowl, combine the apples and 1/4 cup flour. Toss to coat. Pour the apples into pie shell and set aside. In a heavy saucepan over medium heat, stir 1-1/4 cups sugar and 1/4 cup water until the sugar dissolves. Increase the heat and cook, but do not stir, until the mixture turns amber in color. Remove from heat and stir in the 2 Tablespoons of water and 3 Tablespoons of butter (this caramel mixture will bubble quite a lot) until smooth. Immediately pour over the apples in the pie shell. Caramel will harden quickly. Sprinkle cinnamon over the top. In a medium bowl, whisk together flour, 6 Tablespoons sugar, pie spice and salt. Cut butter into small pieces and add to the dry ingredients. Rub in the butter with your hands (as if kneading bread dough) until well blended, then sprinkle the mixture over caramel and apples. Bake for 1 hour and 10 minutes, or until the apples are tender and the topping is golden. (Cover the edge of the crust with foil if browning too quickly.)

Serves: 12

Prep time: 30 minutes
Cook time: 1 hour and 10 minutes (cool for 1 hour before serving)

Chocolate Pecan Pie

This wonderful recipe really is "Easy as pie!" It is great by itself, topped with freshly whipped cream or vanilla ice cream.

1 refrigerated 9" pie crust
1 cup pecan pieces
4 oz. bittersweet chocolate, roughly chopped
3 large eggs
1 cup granulated sugar
1/2 cup (1 stick) unsalted butter, melted
3/4 cup dark corn syrup
1 teaspoon vanilla extract
1/4 teaspoon salt

Let the pie crust sit at room temperature for 15 minutes, then unfold and roll lightly to seal the seams. Press the crust into a glass pie plate and trim any excess dough.

Note: Crust will shrink when baked, so don't trim it too much.

Preheat oven to 350° F. In a small bowl, combine the pecans and chocolate pieces and set aside. In a medium bowl, whisk together all remaining ingredients. Evenly scatter half of the pecan/chocolate mixture in the bottom of the pie shell and top with half of the filling. Repeat with the remaining pecan/chocolate mixture and filling. Bake for 50-55 minutes or until the filling has set and the top has browned; cover just the crust with foil if it browns too quickly. Cool at least 1 hour before serving.

If using a frozen pie crust already in an aluminum tin, or if your pie plate is small, you may have about 1/2 cup of filling left over. Just follow the above instructions and discard excess filling; the pie will still be great!

Serves: 8

Prep time: 20 minutes
Cook time: 50 - 55 minutes (cool for 1 hour before serving)

Do you know why there is no such organization as Chocoholics Anonymous? Because no one wants to quit!

Key Lime Pie

Keep some whipped cream handy for those who want a dollop.

> 1-1/2 cups graham cracker crumbs
> 1 Tablespoon granulated sugar
> 5 Tablespoons butter, melted
> 4 egg yolks, beaten
> 1 can (14 oz.) sweetened condensed milk
> 1/2 cup key lime juice

Preheat oven to 350° F. Mix graham cracker crumbs with sugar and melted butter. Press into 9" pie plate and bake for 5 minutes. Remove from oven and let cool. In medium bowl combine egg yolks, sweetened condensed milk and key lime juice. Mix well. Pour into cooled graham cracker shell. Bake in preheated oven for 18 minutes. Cool and refrigerate until serving.

Serves: 8

 CHILL until serving

 Prep time: 5 minutes
Cook time: 23 minutes

Strawberry Rhubarb Pie

Rhubarb stalks look a lot like red celery, but they're less stringy, very firm, and have a tart flavor.

> 1 refrigerated 9" pie crust
> 2-1/2 cups fresh strawberries, cut into chunks
> 2-1/2 cups fresh rhubarb, cut into small chunks
> 2/3 cup granulated sugar
> 1 teaspoon grated orange zest
> 1/4 cup cornstarch

Bake the pie crust according to the package directions. In a large, heavy saucepan, combine the strawberries, rhubarb, and sugar. Bring to a boil over medium heat, stirring often. Reduce heat slightly, add the orange zest, and cook until rhubarb is soft, about 5 minutes. Meanwhile, whisk together 2 Tablespoons cold water with the cornstarch. When rhubarb is soft, add the cornstarch and stir. Increase the heat again and bring mixture to a boil. Remove from heat and pour into the prepared pie crust. Let cool at room temperature for 30 minutes, then chill for at least 1 hour.

Serves: 8

 Try topping this with vanilla flavored freshly whipped cream or with the Lemon Mousse.

 CHILL at least 1 hour

 Prep time: 45 minutes

Carrot Cake

It's out of this World! See our Cream Cheese Frosting recipe.

2-1/2 cups grated carrots
1-3/4 cups all purpose flour
1 cup granulated sugar
3/4 cup firmly packed brown sugar
1-1/2 teaspoons baking soda
1 teaspoon baking powder
1/2 teaspoon salt
1 teaspoon ground cinnamon
3 eggs
1 cup vegetable oil
1 teaspoon vanilla extract
1 can (8 oz.) crushed pineapple with juice
1 cup chopped walnuts
1 cup raisins

Preheat oven to 350° F. Butter and flour a 9" x 13" pan. In a large bowl, combine grated carrots, flour, sugar, brown sugar, baking soda, baking powder, salt and cinnamon. Stir in eggs, oil, vanilla, pineapple, walnuts, and raisins. Pour batter into prepared pan. Bake for 35 to 40 minutes or until toothpick inserted into center comes out clean. Cool cake before frosting.

Serves: 12 - 16

Prep time: 40 minutes
Cook time: 35 - 40 minutes

Cream Cheese Frosting

Delicious on carrot cake, cupcakes, or fruited breads.

> 3-1/2 cups powdered sugar
> 8 oz. cream cheese
> 1/2 cup margarine, softened
> 1 teaspoon vanilla extract

In a medium bowl, combine powdered sugar, cream cheese, margarine, and vanilla. Beat until smooth. Ready to spread.

Yields: enough to frost one regular cake or 12 - 16 cake squares

 Cream cheese can be replaced by Neufchâtel cheese.

 Prep time: 10 minutes

 <u>CREAM CHEESE</u> (USA): A white soft, smooth, buttery cheese with mild slightly acid taste. Keeps about 2 weeks. Use as a spread, or on crackers.

Cheese Cake

Make this cake a day ahead. The recipe makes a New York style cake . . . more solid and less creamy.

1-1/2 cups graham crackers, crushed
1/3 cup butter, melted
3 packages (8 oz. each) cream cheese, softened
3 eggs
1 can (14 oz.) sweetened condensed milk
1 Tablespoon vanilla extract
2 Tablespoons all purpose flour

Preheat oven to 325° F. Butter a 9" springform pan. In a medium bowl, mix the graham cracker crumbs with melted butter. Press the mixture into the bottom of the springform pan. In a large bowl, combine cream cheese with eggs, sweetened condensed milk, vanilla, and flour. Mix until smooth. Pour filling into prepared crust. Bake for 1 hour. Turn oven off and let cake cool for 2 hours with oven door closed. This prevents cracking. Chill in refrigerator for 6 hours or overnight before removing from pan.

Serves: 12

 CHILL for 6 hours or overnight

 Prep time: 30 minutes, plus stand for 2 hours
Cook time: 1 hour

Individual Raspberry & Chocolate Cakes

If you're a chocoholic, like me, you'll be glad that you only need a cup of chocolate morsels for the cakes, so you should have plenty left over to snack on.

3/4 cup granulated sugar
1/2 cup (1 stick) butter, softened
2 large eggs
1/4 cup evaporated milk
1 teaspoon vanilla extract
1 cup all purpose flour
1/4 teaspoon salt
1 cup fresh raspberries
1 cup semi-sweet chocolate morsels

Preheat oven to 350° F and spray 10 muffin cups. Beat sugar and butter in a large mixing bowl until combined. Add eggs, evaporated milk, and vanilla; beat until blended. Mix in the flour, and salt. Gently fold in the raspberries and chocolate morsels. Spoon batter into the prepared cups and bake for 20-22 minutes or until cakes are golden brown around the edges and top is set. Cool in the pan on a wire rack for 10 minutes. Run a knife around the edges of the cakes to loosen them before removing from the pan to serve.

Serves: 10

 Sprinkle with powdered sugar and serve with a few fresh raspberries on each plate. Or, top the cakes with following recipe for chocolate sauce.

 Cook time: 20 - 22 minutes

Chocolate Sauce

Use this sauce to top Individual Raspberry & Chocolate Cakes, Chocolate Pecan Pie, Chocolate Chip Bundt Cake, or even just ice cream.

3 oz. bittersweet chocolate
6 Tablespoons heavy cream
6 teaspoons unsalted butter

In the top of a double boiler over simmering water, melt the chocolate with the cream and butter. Remove from heat and stir until smooth.

Yields: enough for one regular cake or 10 individual cakes

 If you don't have a double boiler, just bring some water to a low boil in a small saucepan. Stir the sauce ingredients in a small metal bowl while holding it over the water, but be sure to wear an oven mitt.

 Prep time: 10 minutes

 Money talks, but chocolate sings!

Chocolate Chip Bundt Cake

This cake is "from scratch" and super easy to make!

1 cup unsalted butter, softened
2 cups granulated sugar
4 large eggs
3 cups all purpose flour
1/2 teaspoon salt
1/2 teaspoon baking soda
2 Tablespoons unsweetened cocoa
1 cup buttermilk
1/2 teaspoon vanilla extract
1 bag (12 oz.) semi-sweet chocolate chips
1 cup walnut pieces

Preheat the oven to 350° F. Butter and flour a bundt pan and set it aside (cooking spray is <u>not</u> recommended). Beat the butter and the sugar together until creamy, then beat in the eggs. In a separate bowl, sift together the flour, salt, baking soda and cocoa powder. Mix well. Add the dry ingredients alternately with the buttermilk to the butter, sugar and egg mixture. (The batter will be very thick.) Stir in the vanilla, chocolate chips, and walnuts. Spoon the batter into the prepared bundt pan and bake for 55 minutes. Let cool in the pan for 20 minutes, then turn it out onto a serving plate. Sprinkle with powdered sugar, if desired, and serve.

Serves: 12

Prep time: 20 minutes
Cook time: 55 minutes

If you're trying to lose weight, eat a chocolate bar before each meal. That way, it will take the edge off your appetite and you'll eat less!

Mary's Chocolate Cake with Mocha Icing

This cake is rather unusual because it contains no butter or eggs.

Cake:
- 3 cups all purpose flour
- 2 cups granulated sugar
- 6 Tablespoons unsweetened cocoa
- 2 teaspoons baking soda
- 2 cups water
- 3/4 cup vegetable or canola oil
- 2 Tablespoons cider vinegar or white vinegar
- 3 teaspoons vanilla extract

Preheat oven to 350° F and line two 9" round cake pans with parchment paper (or butter and flour them). In a large mixing bowl, combine all the dry ingredients and stir with a whisk to blend well. In a separate bowl, blend the remaining wet ingredients. Add this mixture to the dry ingredients and beat to blend. Pour batter into the prepared pans and bake for 30 minutes. Cool cakes completely in pans, then turn out to frost.

Icing:
- 2 cups powdered sugar
- 1/2 cup (1 stick) unsalted butter, room temperature
- 2 Tablespoons strong hot coffee
- 2 teaspoons unsweetened cocoa
- 1-1/2 teaspoons vanilla extract

Cream together the powdered sugar and softened butter, then add the rest of the ingredients. Use this as filling between the layers of cake and as the frosting on the outside.

Serves: 10 - 12

 It may be difficult, but try not to "sample" too much of the icing since you will need <u>all</u> of it to fill and frost this cake.

 Prep time: 30 minutes
Cook time: 30 minutes

Lemon Bundt Cake

This recipe may seem a little long, but it really comes together very easily and is wonderful accompanied by the Lemon Mousse!

Cake:
3 cups cake flour (such as Wondra® or Swans Down®)
3 teaspoons baking powder
1/2 teaspoon salt
1 cup (2 sticks) unsalted butter, room temperature
1-1/2 cups granulated sugar
4 eggs, beaten
1 cup milk
3 Tablespoons fresh lemon juice
zest of 1 small lemon

Icing:
1/3 cup fresh lemon juice
2 cups powdered sugar
1/2 teaspoon vanilla extract

Generously butter and flour a bundt pan. Preheat oven to 350° F. In a medium bowl, whisk together the cake flour, baking powder, and salt. Use an electric mixer to beat the butter until creamy. Add the sugar, a little at a time, until all is mixed in and smooth (about 5 minutes). Add eggs, one at a time, and continue beating until mixture is thick, fluffy, and doubled in volume (about 5 minutes). With a spatula, fold in 1/3 of the flour mixture then 1/2 cup of milk. Repeat, ending with the last of the flour. Mix in 3 Tablespoons of lemon juice and the lemon zest. Pour batter into the prepared bundt pan and bake in the center of the oven for 45-50 minutes. Let the cake cool, in the pan, for at least 30 minutes since it may not come out of pan in one piece if it has not cooled enough. When cool, turn cake over onto a wire rack with wax paper or foil underneath. In a medium bowl, whisk the icing ingredients together until smooth. Drizzle icing over cake and let stand for 1 hour before serving.

Serves: 12

Prep time: 30 minutes, plus stand 1 hour
Cook time: 45 - 50 minutes

Lemon Mousse

Fair warning: Start this well ahead of time as it takes a while to chill. This is wonderful with the Lemon Bundt Cake or the Strawberry Rhubarb Pie!

10 large egg yolks
1-1/4 cups granulated sugar
3/4 cup fresh lemon juice
1/2 cup (1 stick) unsalted butter, softened and cut into pieces
1 Tablespoon lemon zest
1-1/3 cups heavy cream

In a medium saucepan, whisk together the egg yolks and sugar. Whisk in the lemon juice and pieces of butter. Cook the mixture over medium-low heat, whisking constantly for 6 to 8 minutes (butter should melt, but do not let the mixture boil). Strain the mixture through a fine sieve set over a bowl, then stir in the lemon zest. Cover the mixture with plastic wrap and chill for at least 4 hours or overnight. This yields 2 cups of lemon curd.

As a shortcut, you can use 2 cups of purchased lemon curd instead and then proceed as follows: In a large bowl, beat the heavy cream until stiff peaks form. Gently fold in the lemon curd, 1/2 cup at a time, until it is all incorporated and mixture is smooth.
Cover and chill the mousse at least 4 hours or overnight.

Yields: 5 cups

 CHILL at least 4 hours or overnight

 Prep time: 20 minutes
Cook time: 6 - 8 minutes

Pineapple Upside Down Cake

Easier to make than you think. I promise!

2/3 cup light brown sugar
1/3 cup butter
1 teaspoon vanilla extract
1/2 teaspoon cinnamon
9 slices canned pineapple
9 halves maraschino cherries
2 eggs
1/2 cup granulated sugar
1-1/2 cups all purpose flour
2 teaspoons baking powder
1 teaspoon salt
1/2 cup butter
1/4 cup pineapple juice
1/2 cup buttermilk

Preheat oven to 325° F. Mix the brown sugar and 1/3 cup butter in an ungreased 9" x 9" baking pan. Stir in vanilla and cinnamon. Heat in the oven until brown sugar melts. Arrange pineapple slices over the brown sugar mixture. Place a cherry half in the middle of each slice. In large bowl, mix eggs and sugar. In same bowl, add flour, baking powder, salt, 1/2 cup butter, pineapple juice, and buttermilk. Blend well. Spoon batter into the baking pan. Bake for 35-40 minutes or until an inserted toothpick comes out clean. Invert pan onto platter. Allow it to rest for several minutes before removing.

Serves: 9

Prep time: 45 minutes
Cook time: 35-40 minutes

Pound Cake

This recipe uses a 9" x 5" x 3" loaf pan.
Double the recipe if using a 10" x 4" inch tube pan.

1/2 cup margarine
1-1/2 cups granulated sugar
3 eggs
1/2 cup sour cream
1 teaspoon vanilla extract
1/2 teaspoon baking soda
1-1/2 cups all purpose flour

Preheat oven to 325° F. Beat the margarine and sugar until blended. Mix in eggs, sour cream, and vanilla. Add baking soda and flour, and blend completely. Pour into greased 9" x 5" x 3" loaf pan. Bake for one hour. Cool in pan for 10 minutes. Remove from pan and cool completely on wire rack.

NOTE: If doubling the recipe, bake for 1 hour and 30 minutes.

Serves: 12

Prep time: 20 minutes
Cook time: 1 hour

Pumpkin Cake Squares

If you like pumpkin pie and spice cake, you'll like this cake too.

Cakes:
2 cups granulated sugar
4 large eggs
1 cup vegetable oil
2 cups all purpose flour
2 heaping teaspoons ground cinnamon
1 teaspoon baking powder
1 teaspoon baking soda
1/2 teaspoon salt
1-1/4 cups canned pumpkin

Preheat oven to 350° F and butter two pans – a 9" x 13" <u>and</u> an 8" x 8" metal pan. In a mixer, cream together the sugar, eggs, and oil until well blended. In a separate bowl, whisk together the flour, cinnamon, baking powder, baking soda, and salt. Add the dry ingredients to the wet mixture in 3 additions, mixing well between each. Add the pumpkin last and beat until blended. Pour batter into the prepared pans and bake for 20 to 25 minutes. Let the cakes cool in the pans for 15 minutes, then turn them out onto a cutting board.

Frosting:
4 oz. cream cheese, room temperature
6 Tablespoons unsalted butter, softened
1 Tablespoon milk
1 teaspoon vanilla extract
3 cups powdered sugar

While the cakes continues to cool, beat the cream cheese, butter, milk, and vanilla together. Add the powdered sugar 1/2 cup at a time, beating well after each addition, until all has been added and frosting is smooth and creamy. Be sure the cakes are completely cool before frosting or the icing will melt. Frost just the tops of each cake (not down the sides), then cut them into 1-1/2 inch squares and set them out on a decorative platter or tray.

Prep time: 30 minutes
Cook time: 20 - 25 minutes

Chewy Brownies

Yes Martha . . . I can make great brownies from scratch!

1-2/3 cups granulated sugar
3/4 cup butter, melted
3 eggs
2 teaspoons vanilla extract
1-1/3 cups all purpose flour
3/4 cup unsweetened cocoa
1/2 teaspoon baking powder
1/2 teaspoon salt
1 cup nuts, chopped

Preheat oven to 350° F. In a large bowl, stir sugar and butter together. Add eggs and vanilla. Mix well. Add flour, cocoa, baking powder, and salt to bowl. Mix thoroughly. Stir in nuts. Pour batter into greased 9" x 13" pan. Bake for 20 to 25 minutes or until wooden pick inserted in center comes out slightly sticky. Cool in pan.

Yields: 24

Prep time: 15 minutes
Cook time: 20 - 25 minutes

Warm brownies and ice cream really means "I have a good heart, though my arteries might be a little clogged."

Chocolate Chip Meringues

Fair warning: Although these are very simple to make, they take a long time to mix and bake.

1 cup egg whites (about 5-6 extra large eggs)
2 cups granulated sugar
1 cup <u>mini</u> semi-sweet chocolate morsels

In a standing mixer, whip the egg whites and the sugar together for 30 minutes. Meanwhile, preheat the oven to 350° F and line 3 or 4 cookie sheets with parchment paper. After 30 minutes of continuous beating, the egg whites/sugar should form stiff peaks. Gently fold in the chocolate chips in 3 additions. Place small dollops (no bigger than 1 heaping Tablespoon) onto the lined cookie sheets; dollops can be close together, but not touching. (Cookies will not expand.) Place the cookie sheets in the oven and immediately turn the oven down to 200° F. Leave in the oven, undisturbed, for 4 hours.

Do not use the regular size chocolate morsels as they will sink to the bottoms of the cookies. Food coloring can be added to tint the meringues (i.e.: red or green for gift giving at the holidays).

Yields: 6 dozen cookies

Prep time: 40 minutes
Cook time: 4 hours

Chocolate Chocolate Chip Cookies

Great taste . . . not too rich either.
If you want less chocolate just omit the cocoa.

3/4 cup firmly packed brown sugar
1/2 cup granulated sugar
1 cup margarine
1 teaspoon vanilla extract
2 eggs
2 cups all purpose flour
1/2 cup unsweetened cocoa
1 teaspoon baking soda
1 teaspoon salt
12 oz. semi-sweet chocolate chips

Preheat oven to 375° F. In a large bowl, mix brown sugar, granulated sugar, and margarine. Add vanilla and eggs, and cream all ingredients together. Add flour, cocoa, baking soda, and salt. Mix thoroughly. Stir in chocolate chips. Drop by a Tablespoon of batter 2 inches apart onto an ungreased cookie sheet. Bake for 10 to 13 minutes.

Yields: 48 cookies

 Adding a pinch of salt will enhance the flavor of chocolate recipes.

 Prep time: 15 minutes
Cook time: 10 - 13 minutes

Cookie Bars

A fun and easy treat. Of course, anything made with chocolate is good.

1/2 cup margarine
1-1/2 cups graham cracker crumbs
1 can (14 oz.) sweetened condensed milk
6 oz. semi-sweet chocolate morsels
6 oz. peanut butter morsels
1 cup chopped nuts

Preheat oven to 325° F. In a 9" x 13" baking pan, melt the margarine. Sprinkle the graham cracker crumbs evenly over margarine. Pour sweetened condensed milk evenly over the crumbs. Top with chocolate morsels, peanut butter morsels, and nuts. Press mixture down gently to bind. Bake 25 to 30 minutes until golden. Cool before cutting.

Yields: 24

Prep time: 15 minutes
Cook time: 25 - 30 minutes

Perfect Cookie Cutter Cookies with Frosting

One can only imagine how many cookie cutters Martha has in her collection!

Cookies: 3/4 cup (1-1/2 sticks) unsalted butter, softened
1 cup granulated sugar
1 large egg
1 teaspoon almond (or vanilla) extract
2-1/2 cups all purpose flour
1/2 teaspoon baking soda
1/2 teaspoon salt

Cream together butter and sugar until smooth. Add egg and extract, beating well. In a separate bowl, combine the flour, baking soda and salt, then add to the butter/sugar mixture, beating well. Gather dough in hands and kneed to form a ball, then cover and chill for 1 hour. Let stand at room temperature for about 30 minutes before rolling out on a lightly floured surface to 1/4 inch thickness. Preheat oven to 350° F. Cut out cookies and place 1 inch apart on a parchment lined cookie sheet. Bake for 5 - 6 minutes. Let stand on baking sheet for 5 minutes, then transfer to a wire rack to cool completely. Decorate with frosting.

Frosting: 3 Tablespoons unsalted butter, softened
2-1/4 cups powdered sugar
6 Tablespoons whipping cream
1/4 teaspoon vanilla extract
food coloring (optional)

Beat butter until creamy. Add sugar alternately with cream until well blended. Stir in vanilla. Add food coloring if desired. Icing will be very thick.

Yields: 2-1/2 dozen cookies and 2 cups frosting

 CHILL for 1 hour

 Prep time: 1 hour
Cook time: 5 - 6 minutes

Julia's Fruit Pizza Cookies

Use fresh fruit such as blueberries, bananas, peaches, and/or strawberries. I use them all in different varieties and designs.

20 Sugar Cookies (see our recipe)
8 oz. cream cheese
1/2 cup granulated sugar
1 teaspoon vanilla extract
1/2 cup of desired fruit

In a large bowl, beat the cream cheese with sugar and vanilla. Spread mixture on top of sugar cookies. Arrange desired fruit on top of filling. Chill until serving. You should serve this the same day due to the freshness of fruit.

Serves: 10

 CHILL until serving

 Prep time: 10 minutes

Lemon Shortbread Cookies with Lemon Icing

Consider adding food coloring to lightly tint the icing.

Cookies:
 2 cups all purpose flour
 5 Tablespoons cornstarch
 1/2 teaspoon ground nutmeg
 1/4 teaspoon salt
 1 cup (2 sticks) unsalted butter, room temperature
 2/3 cup granulated sugar
 2 Tablespoons lemon zest
 2 teaspoons vanilla extract

Icing:
 1/2 cup powdered sugar
 4 Tablespoons fresh lemon juice

Preheat oven to 350° F. Combine flour, cornstarch, nutmeg, and salt in a medium bowl. Whisk to blend. In a separate (large) bowl, use an electric mixer to beat butter, sugar, lemon peel, and vanilla until light and fluffy. Add dry ingredients and mix until dough begins to come together. Turn dough onto sheet of waxed paper. Gather dough into a ball; flatten into a disk. Cover with second sheet of waxed paper. Roll out dough to 1/4 inch thickness, then turn and free the bottom and top sheets of paper by turning them over. Cut out cookies using 3-inch cutters. Transfer to an ungreased or parchment paper lined cookie sheet, spacing cookies about 1/2 inch apart. Gather and re-roll scraps; cut out additional cookies until all dough is used. Bake cookies until firm to touch and just beginning to color, about 14 or 15 minutes. Transfer cookies to rack & cool.

In a small bowl, whisk together all of the powdered sugar and just enough of the lemon juice to make a liquid. Drizzle or spoon over cooled cookies, then let icing harden before serving.

Yields: 2 dozen

Prep time: 30 minutes
Cook time: 15 minutes

Oatmeal Raisin Spice Cookies

These super easy cookies get their kick from a box of cake mix.

> 2/3 cup vegetable oil
> 2 large eggs
> 1-1/4 cups quick-cooking oats
>   (not instant or old-fashioned)
> 1 box of spice cake mix (any brand)
> 1/2 cup raisins

Preheat the oven to 350° F and line 2 or 3 cookie sheets with parchment paper. In a large bowl, beat together the oil, eggs, oats, and cake mix. Stir in the raisins. One Tablespoonful at a time, roll the dough into balls in your palm, then press slightly onto the parchment paper. (*You can place them somewhat close together since the cookies will not expand much when baked.) Bake for 8 minutes, or until slightly browned. Transfer cookies to rack and cool.

Yields: 3 dozen

Prep time: 20 minutes
Cook time: 8 minutes

Russian Tea Cakes

I have also seen these cookies labeled Mexican Wedding Cakes;
I'm sure Martha would know their proper name!

1 cup (2 sticks) unsalted butter, softened
1/2 cup powdered sugar, sifted
1-1/2 teaspoons vanilla extract
2-1/4 cups flour
1/4 teaspoon salt
3/4 cup finely chopped walnuts
3 cups powdered sugar

In a large bowl, mix the butter, 1/2 cup powdered sugar, and vanilla thoroughly. In a separate bowl, stir together the flour and salt, then add to the wet mixture. Stir in the nuts and chill the dough for 45 minutes. Preheat oven to 400° F. In your palm, roll dough into 1 inch balls and place on an ungreased cookie sheet. You can set these close together, as cookies will not expand. Bake 8 to 10 minutes. Cookies should set, but not brown. While the cookies are still warm, roll them in powdered sugar. Let them cool, then roll again. Store in an airtight container.

Yields: 4 dozen

 CHILL for 45 minutes

 Try using a 1 inch melon baller to get these cookies just the right size.

 Prep time: 20 minutes
Cook time: 8 - 10 minutes

Sugar Cookies

Tasty alone or as a Fruit Pizza Cookie (see our recipe).

1/2 cup butter, softened
3/4 cup granulated sugar
1 egg
1/2 teaspoon vanilla extract
1-1/4 cups all purpose flour
1/2 teaspoon baking soda
1/4 teaspoon baking powder

Preheat oven to 350° F. In a large bowl, cream together the butter and sugar until smooth. Add egg and vanilla. Blend in the flour, baking soda, and baking powder. Mix well. Roll rounded teaspoonfuls of dough into balls and place onto ungreased cookie sheets yielding 20 cookies. Bake 10 minutes. Cool before removing from cookie sheet.

Yields: 20

Prep time: 15 minutes
Cook time: 10 minutes

Trifecta Cookies

A perfect combination: some peanut butter, a few oats and of course, you gotta have chocolate chips!

1 cup brown sugar
1 cup granulated sugar
3 eggs
1 teaspoon vanilla extract
1 cup margarine
3/4 cup peanut butter
2 cups all purpose flour
1 teaspoon baking soda
1 teaspoon baking powder
3/4 cup oats
12 oz. chocolate chips

Preheat oven to 350° F. In a large bowl mix both sugars, eggs, vanilla, margarine and peanut butter. Add flour, baking soda, baking powder, oats and mix well. Stir in chocolate chips. Drop by the teaspoon onto greased cookie sheet. Bake for 12 to 15 minutes.

Yields: 48 cookies

Prep time: 15 minutes
Cook time: 12 - 15 minutes

English Toffee

To make this, you will need a candy thermometer, which is inexpensive and can be found in most cooking or grocery stores.

1 cup (2 sticks) unsalted butter
1 cup granulated sugar
3 Tablespoons water
1 teaspoon light corn syrup
1-1/2 cups finely chopped almonds, toasted
1 cup milk chocolate chips, slightly warmed

Melt the butter in a heavy saucepan over medium heat. Stir in the sugar, water, and corn syrup until the sugar dissolves. Raise the heat to a boil. Heat, only stirring occasionally, to 290° F on a candy thermometer. When it has reached this temperature it should be a golden, light amber color.
Note: If you stir it too much while it is boiling, the recipe will fail.
Turn off heat and stir in 3/4 cup of almonds. Pour onto an ungreased baking sheet. Sprinkle with the softened chocolate chips, which will melt as you spread the chocolate evenly over the toffee. Sprinkle with the remaining almonds. Refrigerate the toffee to harden. Once cooled, break toffee into chunks and store in an airtight container.

This is another great treat for gift giving at the Holidays.

Prep time: 30 minutes

There is a difference between a cookie sheet and a baking sheet. A cookie sheet is flat to the edge, whereas a baking sheet has low sides (usually only about 3/4" high). Although you can often use either one, for this recipe you must use a baking sheet.

Yvette's Fabulous Fudge

This is a family favorite at the Holidays and is perfect for gift giving.

1 jar (10 oz.) marshmallow cream
1-3/4 cups granulated sugar
1 cup evaporated milk
1/2 cup (1 stick) unsalted butter, melted
1/4 teaspoon salt
1 package (12 oz.) <u>mini</u> semi-sweet chocolate morsels
1 package (11-1/2 oz.) milk chocolate chips
1-1/2 teaspoons vanilla extract
2 cups walnut halves

Butter a 9" x 13" metal or glass pan and set aside. In a large saucepan, combine the marshmallow cream, sugar, milk, butter and salt. Bring to a boil and continue to boil for 5 minutes over medium heat, stirring constantly. Remove from heat, add chocolate morsels and chips, stirring until smooth. Mix the vanilla in well, then add the walnuts. Pour into the prepared pan, cover with plastic wrap, and chill overnight (or until firm). Cut into generous bite size pieces.

Yields: 40 pieces

 CHILL overnight

 Prep time: 20 minutes

 If you have melted chocolate all over your hands, you're eating too slowly!

Ginger Baked Apples

Best topped with whipping cream or vanilla ice cream.

2 large baking apples (such as Rome Beauty)
2 Tablespoons crystallized ginger, chopped
2 Tablespoons butter, melted
6 Tablespoons water
1-1/2 Tablespoons granulated sugar
1-1/2 Tablespoons fresh lemon juice
3/4 teaspoon grated lemon peel
1/2 teaspoon ground cinnamon

Peel the apples halfway down from stem end. Core apples without cutting through the bottom. Place in a broiler-proof and microwave-safe casserole dish. Mix ginger and butter in a small bowl. Spoon half of ginger mixture into hollow of each apple. Stir all remaining ingredients in a small saucepan over medium heat until the sugar dissolves and syrup boils. Pour syrup over apples. Cover casserole dish loosely with plastic wrap, and microwave on high until apples are tender, rotating twice, about 6 minutes. Uncover; spoon juices over. Preheat broiler. Broil apples until tops are glazed and syrup bubbles, about 2 minutes.

Serves: 2

This recipe can easily be doubled.

Prep time: 20 minutes
Cook time: 6 minutes microwave, 2 minutes in broiler

INDEX